One Hundred
and One
Famous Poems

One Hundred
and One
Famous Poems

With a
Prose Supplement

(Revised Edition)

An Anthology Compiled by
ROY J. COOK

Contemporary Books, Inc.
Chicago

Library of Congress Cataloging in Publication Data

101 famous poems.

   Includes index.
   1. English poetry.   2. American poetry.   I. Cook,
Roy, J., 1873–?.   II. Title: One hundred and one famous
poems.   III. Title: One hundred one famous poems.
PR1175.A14   821′.008   81-66883
ISBN 0-8092-5833-1 (deluxe)   AACR2

Published by Contemporary Books, Inc.
180 North Michigan Avenue, Chicago, Illinois 60601
Manufactured in the United States of America
Library of Congress Catalog Card Number: 81-66883
International Standard Book Number: 0-8092-5833-1

Published simultaneously in Canada by
Beaverbooks, Ltd.
150 Lesmill Road
Don Mills, Ontario M3B 2T5
Canada

Preface

This is the age of science, of steel—of speed and the cement road. The age of hard faces and hard highways. Science and steel demand the medium of prose. Speed requires only the look—the gesture. What need then, for poetry?

Great need!

There are souls, in these noise-tired times, that turn aside into unfrequented lanes, where the deep woods have harbored the fragrances of many a blossoming season. Here the light, filtering through perfect forms, arranges itself in lovely patterns for those who perceive beauty.

ROY J. COOK, *Editor.*

Acknowledgments

The selections by Emerson, Burroughs, Holmes, Lowell, Sill, Whittier, Cary, Larcom, and Longfellow are used by permission of and special arrangement with Houghton-Mifflin Company, authorized publishers of their works.

Grateful acknowledgment is also made to D. Appleton & Company, F. W. Bourdillon, Bobbs-Merrill Company, Charles Scribner's Sons, Doubleday-Page & Company, Little, Brown & Company, George H. Doran Company, Lothrop, Lee & Shepard Company, A. P. Watt & Son, *The Academy*, London, and the Librarian, University of Edinburgh, without whose kind cooperation this collection could not have been made.

ROY J. COOK, *Editor.*

Bettmann

The Builders

Henry Wadsworth Longfellow
(Born February 27, 1807; died March 24, 1882)

All are architects of Fate,
   Working in these walls of Time;
Some with massive deeds and great,
   Some with ornaments of rhyme.

Nothing useless is, or low;
   Each thing in its place is best;
And what seems but idle show
   Strengthens and supports the rest.

For the structure that we raise,
   Time is with materials filled;
Our todays and yesterdays
   Are the blocks with which we build.

Truly shape and fashion these;
   Leave no yawning gaps between;
Think not, because no man sees,
   Such things will remain unseen.

In the elder days of Art,
   Builders wrought with greatest care
Each minute and unseen part;
   For the gods see everywhere.

Let us do our work as well,
   Both the unseen and the seen;
Make the house where gods may dwell
   Beautiful, entire, and clean.

Else our lives are incomplete,
   Standing in these walls of Time,
Broken stairways, where the feet
   Stumble, as they seek to climb.

Build today, then, strong and sure,
    With a firm and ample base;
And ascending and secure
    Shall tomorrow find its place.

Thus alone can we attain
    To those turrets, where the eye
Sees the world as one vast plain,
    And one boundless reach of sky.

Bettmann

Opportunity

EDWARD R. SILL

(Born April 29, 1841; died February 27, 1887)

This I beheld, or dreamed it in a dream:—
There spread a cloud of dust along a plain;
And underneath the cloud, or in it, raged
A furious battle, and men yelled, and swords
Shocked upon swords and shields. A prince's banner
Wavered, then staggered backward, hemmed by foes.

A craven hung along the battle's edge,
And thought, "Had I a sword of keener steel—
That blue blade that the king's son bears—but this
Blunt thing!"—he snapped and flung it from his hand.
And lowering crept away and left the field.

Then came the king's son, wounded, sore bestead,
And weaponless, and saw the broken sword,
Hilt-buried in the dry and trodden sand,
And ran and snatched it, and with battle-shout
Lifted afresh he hewed his enemy down,
And saved a great cause that heroic day.

2

Out to Old Aunt Mary's

JAMES WHITCOMB RILEY
(Born October 7, 1849; died July 22, 1916)

Photograph by Mecca Studio

Wasn't it pleasant, O brother mine,
In those old days of the lost sunshine
   Of youth—when the Saturday's chores were through,
   And the "Sunday's wood" in the kitchen, too,
   And we went visiting, "me and you,"
      Out to Old Aunt Mary's?

It all comes back so clear today!
Though I am as bald as you are gray—
   Out by the barn-lot, and down the lane,
   We patter along in the dust again,
   As light as the tips of the drops of the rain,
      Out to Old Aunt Mary's!

We cross the pasture, and through the wood
Where the old gray snag of the poplar stood,
   Where the hammering red-heads hopped awry,
   And the buzzard "raised" in the clearing sky,
   And lolled and circled, as we went by,
      Out to Old Aunt Mary's.

And then in the dust of the road again;
And the teams we met, and the countrymen;
   And the long highway, with sunshine spread
   As thick as butter on country bread,
   Our cares behind, and our hearts ahead
      Out to Old Aunt Mary's.

Why, I see her now in the open door,
Where the little gourds grew up the sides, and o'er
   The clapboard roof!—And her face—ah, me!

3

Wasn't it good for a boy to see—
And wasn't it good for a boy to be
 Out to Old Aunt Mary's?

The jelly—the jam and the marmalade,
And the cherry and quince "preserves" she made!
 And the sweet-sour pickles of peach and pear,
 With cinnamon in 'em, and all things rare!—
 And the more we ate was the more to spare,
  Out to Old Aunt Mary's!

And the old spring-house in the cool green gloom
Of the willow-trees, and the cooler room
 Where the swinging-shelves and the crocks were kept—
 Where the cream in a golden languor slept
 While the waters gurgled and laughed and wept—
  Out to Old Aunt Mary's!

And as many a time have you and I—
Barefoot boys in the days gone by—
 Knelt, and in tremulous ecstasies
 Dipped our lips into sweets like these,—
 Memory now is on her knees
  Out to Old Aunt Mary's!

And O, my brother, so far away,
This is to tell you she waits *today*
 To welcome us:—Aunt Mary fell
 Asleep this morning, whispering, "Tell
 The boys to come!" And all is well
  Out to Old Aunt Mary's!

From *Afterwhiles,* by James Whitcomb Riley.
Copyright 1898. Used by special permission of
the publishers, the Bobbs-Merrill Company.

The complete edition of Riley's poems in-
cludes many stanzas which are familiar only to
the student of Riley's poems. Most editors omit
the next to the last stanza, as the poem stands
complete, but it is the opinion of Prof. R. M.
Alden of Stanford University that with this
omission the continuity of thought is broken.

Bettmann

Each and All

RALPH WALDO EMERSON
(Born May 25, 1803; died April 27, 1882)

Little thinks, in the field, yon red-cloaked clown
Of thee from the hill-top looking down;
The heifer that lows in the upland farm,
Far-heard, lows not thine ear to charm;
The sexton, tolling his bell at noon,
Deems not that great Napoleon
Stops his horse, and lists with delight,
Whilst his files sweep round yon Alpine height;
Nor knowest thou what argument
Thy life to thy neighbor's creed has lent.
All are needed by each one,—
Nothing is fair or good alone.
I thought the sparrow's note from heaven,
Singing at dawn on the alder bough;
I brought him home, in his nest, at even;
He sings the song, but it cheers not now;
For I did not bring home the river and sky;
He sang to my ear,—they sang to my eye.

The delicate shells lay on the shore;
The bubbles of the latest wave
Fresh pearls to their enamel gave,
And the bellowing of the savage sea
Greeted their safe escape to me.
I wiped away the weeds and foam—
I fetched my sea-born treasures home;
But the poor, unsightly, noisome things
Had left their beauty on the shore
With the sun and the sand and the wild uproar.

The lover watched his graceful maid,
As 'mid the virgin train she strayed,
Nor knew her beauty's best attire

5

Was woven still by the snow-white choir.
At last she came to his hermitage,
Like the bird from the woodlands to the cage;
The gay enchantment was undone—
A gentle wife, but fairy none.

Then I said, "I covet truth;
Beauty is unripe childhood's cheat;
I leave it behind with the games of youth."
As I spoke, beneath my feet
The ground-pine curled its pretty wreath,
Running over the club-moss burrs;
I inhaled the violet's breath;
Around me stood the oaks and firs;
Pine cones and acorns lay on the ground;
Over me soared the eternal sky,
Full of light and of deity;
Again I saw, again I heard,
The rolling river, the morning bird;
Beauty through my senses stole;
I yielded myself to the perfect whole.

Bettmann

The Rhodora
On Being Asked
Whence Is the Flower

RALPH WALDO EMERSON
(Born May 25, 1803; died April 27, 1882)

In May, when sea-winds pierced our solitudes,
I found the fresh Rhodora in the woods,
Spreading its leafless blooms in a damp nook,
To please the desert and the sluggish brook.
The purple petals, fallen in the pool,
Made the black water with their beauty gay;
Here might the redbird come his plumes to cool,
And court the flower that cheapens his array.
Rhodora! if the sages ask thee why
This charm is wasted on the earth and sky,
Tell them, dear, that if eyes were made for seeing
Then Beauty is its own excuse for being:
Why thou wert there, O rival of the rose!
I never thought to ask, I never knew:
But, in my simple ignorance, suppose
The self-same Power that brought me there brought you.

Bettmann

Charge of the Light Brigade

ALFRED TENNYSON
(First Baron)
(Born August 6, 1809; died October 6, 1892)

Half a league, half a league,
Half a league onward,
All in the valley of Death
    Rode the six hundred.
"Forward, the Light Brigade!
Charge for the guns!" he said:
Into the valley of Death
    Rode the six hundred.

"Forward, the Light Brigade!"
Was there a man dismayed?
Not tho' the soldiers knew
    Someone had blundered:
Theirs not to make reply,
Theirs not to reason why,
Theirs but to do and die:
Into the valley of Death
    Rode the six hundred.

Cannon to right of them,
Cannon to left of them,
Cannon in front of them
    Volleyed and thunder'd;
Storm'd at with shot and shell,
Boldly they rode and well,
Into the jaws of Death,
Into the mouth of Hell,
    Rode the six hundred.

Flashed all their sabres bare,
Flashed as they turned in air,
Sab'ring the gunners there,

8

Charging an army, while
  All the world wondered:
Plunged in the battery smoke,
Right through the line they broke;
Cossack and Russian
Reeled from the sabre-stroke
  Shattered and sundered.
Then they rode back, but not—
  Not the six hundred.

Cannon to right of them,
Cannon to left of them,
Cannon behind them
  Volleyed and thundered;
Stormed at with shot and shell,
While horse and hero fell,
They that had fought so well
Came thro' the jaws of Death,
Back from the mouth of Hell,
All that was left of them,
  Left of six hundred.

When can their glory fade?
Oh, the wild charge they made!
  All the world wondered.
Honor the charge they made!
Honor the Light Brigade,
  Noble Six Hundred!

The Night Has a Thousand Eyes

FRANCIS WILLIAM BOURDILLON
(Born March 22, 1852; died January 13, 1921)

The night has a thousand eyes,
    And the day but one;
Yet the light of the bright world dies
    With the dying sun.

The mind has a thousand eyes,
    And the heart but one;
Yet the light of a whole life dies
    When love is done.

The House by the Side of the Road

SAM WALTER FOSS
(Born June 19, 1858; died February 26, 1911)

"He was a friend to man, and he lived
In a house by the side of the road."—*Homer*

There are hermit souls that live withdrawn
    In the place of their self-content;
There are souls like stars, that dwell apart,
    In a fellowless firmament;
There are pioneer souls that blaze their paths
    Where highways never ran—
But let me live by the side of the road
    And be a friend to man.

Let me live in a house by the side of the road,
    Where the race of men go by—

The men who are good and the men who are bad,
  As good and as bad as I.
I would not sit in the scorner's seat,
  Or hurl the cynic's ban—
Let me live in a house by the side of the road
  And be a friend to man.

I see from my house by the side of the road,
  By the side of the highway of life,
The men who press with the ardor of hope,
  The men who are faint with the strife.
But I turn not away from their smiles nor their tears,
  Both parts of an infinite plan—
Let me live in a house by the side of the road
  And be a friend to man.

I know there are brook-gladdened meadows ahead
  And mountains of wearisome height;
That the road passes on through the long afternoon
  And stretches away to the night.
But still I rejoice when the travelers rejoice.
  And weep with the strangers that moan,
Nor live in my house by the side of the road
  Like a man who dwells alone.

Let me live in my house by the side of the road—
  It's here the race of men go by.
They are good, they are bad, they are weak, they are strong,
  Wise, foolish—so am I;
Then why should I sit in the scorner's seat,
  Or hurl the cynic's ban?
Let me live in my house by the side of the road
  And be a friend to man.

Used by special arrangement with the publishers, Lothrop, Lee & Shepard Co.

I Have a Rendezvous with Death

Alan Seeger
(Born June 22, 1888; died July 4, 1916)

I have a rendezovous with Death
  At some disputed barricade
  When Spring comes round with
    rustling shade
And apple blossoms fill the air.
  I have a rendezvous with Death
When Spring brings back blue days and fair.

It may be he shall take my hand
And lead me into his dark land
  And close my eyes and quench my breath;
It may be I shall pass him still.
  I have a rendezvous with Death
On some scarred slope of battered hill,
  When Spring comes round again this year
  And the first meadow flowers appear.

God knows 'twere better to be deep
    Pillowed in silk and scented down,
Where love throbs out in blissful sleep,
  Pulse nigh to pulse, and breath to breath,
Where hushed awakenings are dear . . .
  But I've a rendezvous with Death
    At midnight in some flaming town,
When Spring trips north again this year,
  And I to my pledged word am true,
  I shall not fail that rendezvous.

One of the greatest poems written during the
First World War. From *Poems by Alan Seeger*,
Copyright 1916, by Charles Scribner's Sons.

In Flanders Fields

Bettmann

LIEUT.-COL. JOHN McCRAE

(Born November 30, 1872; died January 28, 1918)

The author of this poem, a member of the first Canadian contingent, died in France after four years of medical service on the western front.

In Flanders fields the poppies blow
Between the crosses, row on row,
   That mark our place; and in the sky
   The larks, still bravely singing, fly
Scarce heard amid the guns below.

We are the Dead. Short days ago
We lived, felt dawn, saw sunset glow,
   Loved and were loved, and now we lie
      In Flanders fields.

Take up our quarrel with the foe;
To you from failing hands we throw
   The torch; be yours to hold it high.
   If ye break faith with us who die
We shall not sleep, though poppies grow
      In Flanders fields.

By courtesy of *Punch*.

Moonlight

From "The Merchant of Venice"

WILLIAM SHAKESPEARE
(Born April 23[?], 1564; died April 23, 1616)

How sweet the moonlight sleeps upon this bank!
Here will we sit, and let the sound of music
Creep in our ears: soft stillness, and the night,
Become the touches of sweet harmony.

Sit, Jessica: look, how the floor of heaven
Is thick inlaid with patines of bright gold:
There's not the smallest orb which thou behold'st,
But in his motion like an angel sings,
Still quiring to the young-ey'd cherubims.

Bettmann

O Captain!
My Captain!

WALT WHITMAN
(Born May 31, 1819; died March 26, 1892)

O Captain! my Captain! our fearful trip is done;
The ship has weather'd every rack, the prize we sought is won;
The port is near, the bells I hear, the people all exulting,
While follow eyes the steady keel, the vessel grim and daring:

But O heart! heart! heart!
O the bleeding drops of red,
Where on the deck my Captain lies,
Fallen cold and dead.

O Captain! my Captain! rise up and hear the bells;
Rise up—for you the flag is flung—for you the bugle trills;
For you bouquets and ribbon'd wreaths—for you the shores
    a-crowding;
For you they call, the swaying mass, their eager faces turning:

    Here Captain! dear father!
      This arm beneath your head;
        It is some dream that on the deck
          You've fallen cold and dead.

My Captain does not answer, his lips are pale and still;
My father does not feel my arm, he has no pulse or will;
The ship is anchor'd safe and sound, its voyage closed and done;
From fearful trip the victor ship comes in with object won:

    Exult, O shores, and ring, O bells!
      But I, with mournful tread,
        Walk the deck my Captain lies,
          Fallen cold and dead.

The
Chambered Nautilus

OLIVER WENDELL HOLMES
(Born August 29, 1809; died October 7, 1894)

Bettmann

This is the ship of pearl which, poets feign,
    Sails the unshadowed main,—
    The venturous bark that flings
On the sweet summer wind its purpled wings
In gulfs enchanted, where the Siren sings,
    And coral reefs lie bare,
Where the cold sea-maids rise to sun their streaming hair.

Its webs of living gauze no more unfurl;
    Wrecked is the ship of pearl!

And every chambered cell,
Where its dim dreaming life was wont to dwell,
As the frail tenant shaped his growing shell,
    Before thee lies revealed,—
Its irised ceiling rent, its sunless crypt unsealed!

Year after year beheld the silent toil
    That spread his lustrous coil;
    Still, as the spiral grew,
He left the past year's dwelling for the new,
Stole with soft step its shining archway through,
    Built up its idle door,
Stretched in his last-found home, and knew the old no more.

Thanks for the heavenly message brought by thee,
    Child of the wandering sea,
    Cast from her lap, forlorn!
From thy dead lips a clearer note is born
Than ever Triton blew from wreathèd horn!
    While on mine ear it rings,
Through the deep caves of thought I hear a voice that
        sings:—

Build thee more stately mansions, O my soul,
    As the swift seasons roll!
    Leave thy low-vaulted past!
Let each new temple, nobler than the last,
Shut thee from heaven with a dome more vast,
    Till thou at length art free,
Leaving thine outgrown shell by life's unresting sea!

Bettmann

Christmas Everywhere

PHILLIPS BROOKS
(Born December 13, 1835; died January 23, 1893)

Everywhere, everywhere, Christmas tonight!
Christmas in lands of the fir-tree and pine,
Christmas in lands of the palm-tree and vine,
Christmas where snow peaks stand solemn and white,
Christmas where cornfields stand sunny and bright.
Christmas where children are hopeful and gay,
Christmas where old men are patient and gray,
Christmas where peace, like a dove in his flight,
Broods o'er brave men in the thick of the fight;
Everywhere, everywhere, Christmas tonight!

For the Christ-child who comes is the Master of all;
No palace too great, no cottage too small.

Bettmann

Little Boy Blue

EUGENE FIELD
(Born September 3, 1850; died November 4, 1895)

The little toy dog is covered with dust,
But sturdy and stanch he stands;
And the little toy soldier is red with rust,
And his musket moulds in his hands.
Time was when the little toy dog was new,
And the soldier was passing fair,
And that was the time when our Little Boy Blue
Kissed them and put them there.

"Now, don't you go till I come," he said,
"And don't you make any noise!"
So toddling off to his trundle-bed
He dreamt of the pretty toys.
And as he was dreaming, an angel song
Awakened our Little Boy Blue,—
Oh, the years are many, the years are long,
But the little toy friends are true!

Ay, faithful to Little Boy Blue they stand,
Each in the same old place,
Awaiting the touch of a little hand,
The smile of a little face.
And they wonder, as waiting these long years through,
In the dust of that little chair,
What has become of our Little Boy Blue
Since he kissed them and put them there.

From *The Poems of Eugene Field.* Copyright
1911, Charles Scribner's Sons.

Bettmann

The Daffodils

WILLIAM WORDSWORTH
(Born April 7, 1770; died April 23, 1850)

I wandered lonely as a cloud
    That floats on high o'er vales and hills,
When all at once I saw a crowd,
    A host, of golden daffodils;
Beside the lake, beneath the trees,
Fluttering and dancing in the breeze.

Continuous as the stars that shine
    And twinkle on the milky way,
They stretched in never-ending line
    Along the margin of a bay:
Ten thousand saw I at a glance,
Tossing their heads in sprightly dance.

The waves beside them danced; but they
    Outdid the sparkling waves in glee:
A poet could not but be gay,
    In such a jocund company:
I gazed—and gazed—but little thought
What wealth the show to me had brought:

For oft, when on my couch I lie
    In vacant or in pensive mood,
They flash upon that inward eye
    Which is the bliss of solitude;
And then my heart with pleasure fills,
And dances with the daffodils.

Bettmann

June

From "The Vision of Sir Launfal"

JAMES RUSSELL LOWELL

(Born February 22, 1819; died August 12, 1891)

Over his keys the musing organist,
  Beginning doubtfully and far away,
First lets his fingers wander as they list,
  And builds a bridge from Dreamland for his lay:
Then, as the touch of his loved instrument
  Gives hope and fervor, nearer draws his theme,
First guessed by faint auroral flushes sent
  Along the wavering vista of his dream.

    Not only around our infancy
    Doth heaven with all its splendors lie;
    Daily, with souls that cringe and plot,
    We Sinais climb and know it not.

Over our manhood bend the skies;
  Against our fallen and traitor lives
The great winds utter prophecies;
  With our faint hearts the mountain strives;
Its arms outstretched, the druid wood
  Waits with its benedicite;
And to our age's drowsy blood
  Still shouts the inspiring sea.

Earth gets its price for what Earth gives us;
  The beggar is taxed for a corner to die in,
The priest hath his fee who comes and shrives us,
  We bargain for the graves we lie in;
At the devil's booth are all things sold,
Each ounce of dross costs its ounce of gold;
For a cap and bells our lives we pay,
  Bubbles we buy with a whole soul's tasking;
'Tis heaven alone that is given away,

20

'Tis only God may be had for the asking;
No price is set on the lavish summer;
June may be had by the poorest comer.

And what is so rare as a day in June?
   Then, if ever, come perfect days;
Then Heaven tries earth if it be in tune,
   And over it softly her warm ear lays;
Whether we look, or whether we listen,
We hear life murmur, or see it glisten;
Every clod feels a stir of might,
   An instinct within it that reaches and towers,
And, groping blindly above it for light,
   Climbs to a soul in grass and flowers;
The flush of life may well be seen
   Thrilling back over hills and valleys;
The cowslip startles in meadows green,
   The buttercup catches the sun in its chalice,
And there's never a leaf nor a blade too mean
   To be some happy creature's palace;
The little bird sits at his door in the sun,
   Atilt like a blossom among the leaves,
And lets his illumined being o'errun
   With the deluge of summer it receives;
His mate feels the eggs beneath her wings,
And the heart in her dumb breast flutters and sings;
He sings to the wide world and she to her nest—
In the nice ear of Nature, which song is the best?

Now is the high-tide of the year,
   And whatever of life hath ebbed away
Comes flooding back with a ripply cheer,
   Into every bare inlet and creek and bay;
Now the heart is so full that a drop overfills it,
We are happy now because God wills it;
No matter how barren the past may have been,
'Tis enough for us now that the leaves are green;
We sit in the warm shade and feel right well
How the sap creeps up and the blossoms swell;
We may shut our eyes, but we cannot help knowing
That skies are clear and grass is growing;
The breeze comes whispering in our ear,
That dandelions are blossoming near,
   That maize has sprouted, that streams are flowing,
That the river is bluer than the sky,

That the robin is plastering his house hard by;
And if the breeze kept the good news back,
For other couriers we should not lack;
   We could guess it all by yon heifer's lowing,—
And hark! how clear bold chanticleer,
Warmed with the new wine of the year,
   Tells all in his lusty, crowing!

Bettmann

Ode to the West Wind

PERCY BYSSHE SHELLEY
(Born August 4, 1792; died July 8, 1822)

O wild West Wind, thou breath of Autumn's being,
   Thou, from whose unseen presence the leaves dead
Are driven, like ghosts from an enchanter fleeing,
   Yellow, and black, and pale, and hectic red,
Pestilence-stricken multitudes: O thou,
   Who chariotest to their dark wintry bed
The winged seeds, where they lie cold and low,
   Each like a corpse within its grave, until
Thine azure sister of the Spring shall blow
   Her clarion o'er the dreaming earth, and fill
(Driving sweet buds like flocks to feed in air)
   With living hues and odors plain and hill:
Wild Spirit, which art moving everywhere;
Destroyer and preserver; hear, oh hear!

Thou on whose stream, mid the steep sky's commotion,
   Loose clouds like earth's decaying leaves are shed,
Shook from the tangled boughs of Heaven and Ocean,
   Angels of rain and lightning: there are spread
On the blue surface of thine aëry surge,
   Like the bright hair uplifted from the head

Of some fierce Maenad, even from the dim verge
  Of the horizon to the zenith's height,
The locks of the approaching storm. Thou dirge
  Of the dying year, to which this closing night
Will be the dome of a vast sepulchre,
  Vaulted with all thy congregated might
Of vapours, from whose solid atmosphere
Black rain, and fire, and hail will burst: oh, hear!

Thou who didst waken from his summer dreams
  The blue Mediterranean, where he lay,
Lulled by the coil of his crystalline streams,
  Beside a pumice isle in Baiae's bay,
And saw in sleep old palaces and towers
  Quivering within the wave's intenser day,
All overgrown with azure moss and flowers
  So sweet, the sense faints picturing them! Thou
For whose path the Atlantic's level powers
  Cleave themselves into chasms, while far below
The sea-blooms and the oozy woods which wear
  The sapless foliage of the ocean, know
Thy voice, and suddenly grow gray with fear,
And tremble and despoil themselves: oh, hear!

If I were a dead leaf thou mightest bear;
  If I were a swift cloud to fly with thee;
A wave to pant beneath thy power, and share
  The impulse of thy strength, only less free
Than Thou, O uncontrollable! If even
  I were as in my boyhood, and could be
The comrade of thy wanderings over Heaven,
  As then, when to outstrip thy skiey speed
Scarce seem'd a vision; I would ne'er have striven
  As thus with thee in prayer in my sore need.
Oh, lift me as a wave, a leaf, a cloud!
  I fall upon the thorns of life! I bleed!
A heavy weight of hours has chained and bowed
One too like thee: tameless, and swift, and proud.

Make my thy lyre, even as the forest is:
  What if my leaves are falling like its own!
The tumult of thy mighty harmonies
  Will take from both a deep, autumnal tone,
Sweet though in sadness. Be thou, Spirit fierce,
  My spirit! be thou me, impetuous one!

23

Drive my dead thoughts over the universe,
  Like withered leaves to quicken a new birth!
And, by the incantation of this verse,
  Scatter, as from an unextinguished hearth
Ashes and sparks, my words among mankind!
  Be through my lips to unawakened earth
The trumpet of a prophecy! O, Wind,
If Winter comes, can Spring be far behind?

Bettmann

The Snowstorm

RALPH WALDO EMERSON
(Born May 25, 1803; died April 27, 1882)

Announced by all the trumpets of the sky,
Arrives the snow, and, driving o'er the fields,
Seems nowhere to alight: the whited air
Hides hills and woods, the river, and the heaven,
And veils the farmhouse at the garden's end.
The sled and traveler stopped, the courier's feet
Delayed, all friends shut out, the housemates sit
Around the radiant fireplace, enclosed
In a tumultuous privacy of storm.

Come, see the north wind's masonry.
Out of an unseen quarry evermore
Furnished with tile, the fierce artificer
Curves his white bastions with projected roof
Round every windward stake or tree or door.
Speeding, the myriad-handed, his wild work
So fanciful, so savage, naught cares he
For number or proportion. Mockingly
On coop or kennel he hangs Parian wreaths;
A swan-like fórm invests the hidden thorn;

Fills up the farmer's lane from wall to wall,
Maugre the farmer's sighs; and at the gate
A tapering turret overtops the work.
And when his hours are numbered, and the world
Is all his own, retiring, as he were not,
Leaves, when the sun appears, astonished Art
To mimic in slow structures, stone by stone,
Built in an age, the mad wind's night-work,
The frolic architecture of the snow.

Bettmann

To a Skylark

PERCY BYSSHE SHELLEY
(Born August 4, 1792; died July 8, 1822)

Hail to thee, blithe spirit!
Bird thou never wert,
That from heaven, or near it,
Pourest thy full heart
In profuse strains of unpremeditated art.

Higher still and higher
From the earth thou springest,
Like a cloud of fire;
The blue deep thou wingest,
And singing still dost soar, and soaring ever singest.

In the golden lightning
Of the sunken sun,
O'er which clouds are brightening,
Thou dost float and run,
Like an unbodied joy whose race is just begun.

The pale purple even
Melts around thy flight;

Like a star of heaven,
In the broad daylight
Thou art unseen, but yet I hear thy shrill delight,

Keen as are the arrows
Of that silver sphere,
Whose intense lamp narrows
In the white dawn clear,
Until we hardly see, we feel that it is there.

All the earth and air
With thy voice is loud,
As, when night is bare,
From one lonely cloud
The moon rains out her beams, and heaven is overflowed.

What thou art we know not;
What is most like thee?
From rainbow clouds there flow not
Drops so bright to see,
As from thy presence showers a rain of melody.

Like a poet hidden
In the light of thought,
Singing hymns unbidden,
Till the world is wrought
To sympathy with hopes and fears it heeded not;

Like a high-born maiden
In a palace tower,
Soothing her love-laden
Soul in secret hour
With music sweet as love, which overflows her bower;

Like a glow-worm golden
In a dell of dew,
Scattering unbeholden
Its aerial hue
Among the flowers and grass, which screen it from the view;

Like a rose embowered
In its own green leaves,
By winds deflowered,
Till the scent it gives
Makes faint with too much sweet these heavy-wingèd thieves.

Sound of vernal showers,
On the twinkling grass,
Rain-awakened flowers,
All that ever was
Joyous and clear and fresh thy music doth surpass.

Teach us, sprite or bird,
What sweet thoughts are thine!
I have never heard
Praise of love or wine
That panted forth a flood of rapture so divine.

Chorus hymeneal
Or triumphal chant,
Matched with thine, would be all
But an empty vaunt,—
A thing wherein we feel there is some hidden want.

What objects are the fountains
Of thy happy strain?
What fields or waves or mountains?
What shapes of sky or plain?
What love of thine own kind? what ignorance of pain?

With thy clear keen joyance
Languor cannot be;
Shadow of annoyance
Never came near thee;
Thou lovest, but ne'er knew love's sad satiety.

Waking or asleep,
Thou of death must deem
Things more true and deep
Than we mortals dream,
Oh how could thy notes flow in such a crystal stream?

We look before and after,
And pine for what is not;
Our sincerest laughter
With some pain is fraught;
Our sweetest songs are those that tell of saddest thought.

Yet if we could scorn
Hate and pride and fear;
If we were things born

Not to shed a tear,
I know not how thy joy we ever should come near.

Better than all measures
Of delightful sound,
Better than all treasures
That in books are found,
Thy skill to poet were, thou scorner of the ground!

Teach me half the gladness
That thy brain must know,
Such harmonious madness
From my lips would flow,
The world should listen then, as I am listening now.

Bettmann

Hiawatha's Childhood

HENRY WADSWORTH LONGFELLOW
(Born February 27, 1807; died March 24, 1882)

By the shores of Gitche Gumee,
By the shining Big-Sea-Water,
Stood the wigwam of Nokomis,
Daughter of the Moon, Nokomis.
Dark behind it rose the forest,
Rose the black and gloomy pine-trees,
Rose the firs with cones upon them;
Bright before it beat the water,
Beat the clear and sunny water,
Beat the shining Big-Sea-Water.
    There the wrinkled old Nokomis
Nursed the little Hiawatha,
Rocked him in his linden cradle,
Bedded soft in moss and rushes,
Safely bound with reindeer sinews;
Stilled his fretful wail by saying,

"Hush! the Naked Bear will hear thee!"
Lulled him into slumber, singing,
"Ewa-yea! my little owlet!
Who is this, that lights the wigwam?
With his great eyes lights the wigwam?
Ewa-yea! my little owlet!"
   Many things Nokomis taught him
Of the stars that shine in heaven;
Showed him Ishkoodah, the comet,
Ishkoodah, with fiery tresses;
Showed the Death-Dance of the spirits,
Warriors with their plumes and war-clubs,
Flaring far away to northward
In the frosty nights of winter;
Showed the broad white road in heaven,
Pathway of the ghosts, the shadows,
Running straight across the heavens,
Crowded with the ghosts, the shadows.
   At the door on summer evenings,
Sat the little Hiawatha;
Heard the whispering of the pine-trees,
Heard the lapping of the waters,
Sounds of music, words of wonder;
"Minne-wawa!" said the pine-trees,
"Mudway-aushka!" said the water.
   Saw the fire-fly Wah-wah-taysee,
Flitting through the dusk of evening,
With the twinkle of its candle
Lighting up the brakes and bushes,
And he sang the song of children,
Sang the song Nokomis taught him:
"Wah-wah-taysee, little fire-fly,
Little flitting, white-fire insect,
Little, dancing, white-fire creature,
Light me with your little candle,
Ere upon my bed I lay me,
Ere in sleep I close my eyelids!"
   Saw the moon rise from the water,
Rippling, rounding from the water,
Saw the flecks and shadows on it,
Whispered, "What is that, Nokomis?"
And the good Nokomis answered:
"Once a warrior, very angry,
Seized his grandmother, and threw her
Up into the sky at midnight;

Right against the moon he threw her;
'Tis her body that you see there."
   Saw the rainbow in the heaven,
In the eastern sky the rainbow,
Whispered, "What is that, Nokomis?"
And the good Nokomis answered:
" 'Tis the heaven of flowers you see there;
All the wild-flowers of the forest,
All the lilies of the prairie,
When on earth they fade and perish,
Blossom in that heaven above us."
   When he heard the owls at midnight,
Hooting, laughing in the forest,
"What is that?" he cried in terror;
"What is that," he said, "Nokomis?"
And the good Nokomis answered:
"That is but the owl and owlet,
Talking in their native language,
Talking, scolding at each other."
   Then the little Hiawatha
Learned of every bird its language,
Learned their names and all their secrets,
How they built their nests in summer,
Where they hid themselves in winter,
Talked with them whene'er he met them,
Called them "Hiawatha's Chickens."
   Of all beasts he learned the language,
Learned their names and all their secrets,
How the beavers built their lodges,
Where the squirrels hid their acorns,
How the reindeer ran so swiftly,
Why the rabbit was so timid,
Talked with them whene'er he met them,
Called them "Hiawatha's Brothers."

Bettmann

The Happy Warrior

WILLIAM WORDSWORTH

(Born April 7, 1770; died April 23, 1850)

Who is the happy Warrior? Who is he
That every man in arms should wish to be?
—It is the generous Spirit, who, when brought
Among the tasks of real life, hath wrought
Upon the plan that pleased his boyish thought:
Whose high endeavors are an inward light
That makes the path before him always bright:
Who, with a natural instinct to discern
What knowledge can perform, is diligent to learn;
Abides by this resolve, and stops not there,
But makes his moral being his prime care;
Who, doomed to go in company with Pain,
And Fear, and Bloodshed, miserable train!
Turns his necessity to glorious gain;
In face of these doth exercise a power
Which is our human nature's highest dower;
Controls them and subdues, transmutes, bereaves
Of their bad influence, and their good receives:
By objects, which might force the soul to abate
Her feeling, rendered more compassionate;
Is placable—because occasions rise
So often that demand such sacrifice;
More skillful in self-knowledge, even more pure,
As tempted more; more able to endure,
As more exposed to suffering and distress;
Thence also, more alive to tenderness.
—'Tis he whose law is reason; who depends
Upon that law as on the best of friends;
Whence, in a state where men are tempted still
To evil for a guard against worse ill,
And what in quality or act is best
Doth seldom on a right foundation rest,

31

He labors good on good to fix, and owes
To virtue every triumph that he knows:
—Who, if he rise to station of command,
Rises by open means; and there will stand
On honorable terms, or else retire,
And in himself possess his own desire;
Who comprehends his trust, and to the same
Keeps faithful with a singleness of aim;
And therefore does not stoop, nor lie in wait
For wealth, or honors, or for worldly state;
Whom they must follow; on whose head must fall,
Like showers of manna, if they come at all:
Whose powers shed round him in the common strife,
Or mild concerns of ordinary life,
A constant influence, a peculiar grace;
But who, if he be called upon to face
Some awful moment to which Heaven has joined
Great issues, good or bad for human kind,
Is happy as a Lover; and attired
With sudden brightness, like a Man inspired;
And, through the heat of conflict, keeps the law
In calmness made, and sees what he foresaw;
Or if an unexpected call succeed,
Come when it will, is equal to the need:
—He who, though thus endued as with a sense
And faculty for storm and turbulence,
Is yet a Soul whose master-bias leans
To homefelt pleasures and to gentle scenes;
Sweet images! which, wheresoe'er he be,
Are at his heart; and such fidelity
It is his darling passion to approve;
More brave for this, that he hath much to love:—
'Tis, finally, the Man who lifted high,
Conspicuous object in a Nation's eye,
Or left unthought-of in obscurity,—
Who, with a toward or untoward lot,
Prosperous or adverse, to his wish or not—
Plays, in the many games of life, that one
Where what he most doth value must be won:
Whom neither shape of danger can dismay,
Nor thought of tender happiness betray;
Who, not content that former worth stand fast,
Looks forward, persevering to the last,
From well to better, daily self-surpast;

Who, whether praise of him must walk the earth
Forever, and to noble deeds give birth,
Or he must fall, to sleep without his fame,
And leave a dead unprofitable name—
Finds comfort in himself and in his cause;
And, while the mortal mist is gathering, draws
His breath in confidence of Heaven's applause:
This is the happy Warrior; this is He
That every Man in arms should wish to be.

Bettmann

Ann Rutledge

EDGAR LEE MASTERS
(Born August 23, 1869; died March 5, 1950)

Out of me unworthy and unknown
The vibrations of deathless music;
"With malice toward none, with charity for all."
Out of me the forgiveness of millions toward millions,
And the beneficent face of a nation
Shining with justice and truth.
I am Ann Rutledge who sleeps beneath these weeds,
Beloved in life of Abraham Lincoln,
Wedded to him, not through union,
But through separation.
Bloom forever, O Republic,
From the dust of my bosom!

From *Spoon River Anthology*, by Edgar Lee
Masters, and published by the Macmillan
Company. Copyright 1916. By special permission of the author and publisher.

33

Bettmann

Grass

CARL SANDBURG
*(Born Galesburg, Illinois, 1872;
died July 22, 1967)*

Pile the bodies high at Austerlitz and Waterloo.
Shovel them under and let me work—
      I am the grass; I cover all.

And pile them high at Gettysburg
And pile them high at Ypres and Verdun.
Shovel them under and let me work.
Two years, ten years, and passengers ask the conductor:
      What place is this?
      Where are we now?

      I am the grass.
      Let me work.

From *Cornhuskers*, by Carl Sandburg. Copyright 1918. Published by Henry Holt & Co. Special permission of the publisher.

Not in Vain

EMILY DICKINSON
(Born 1830; died 1886)

If I can stop one heart from breaking,
I shall not live in vain:
If I can ease one life the aching,
Or cool one pain,
Or help one fainting robin
Unto his nest again,
I shall not live in vain.

Bettmann

Sheridan's Ride

THOMAS BUCHANAN READ
(Born March 12, 1822; died May 11, 1872)

Up from the South at break of day,
Bringing to Winchester fresh dismay,
The affrighted air with a shudder bore,
Like a herald in haste, to the chieftain's door,
The terrible grumble, and rumble, and roar,
Telling the battle was on once more,
    And Sheridan twenty miles away.

And wider still those billows of war
Thundered along the horizon's bar;
And louder yet into Winchester rolled
The roar of that red sea uncontrolled,
Making the blood of the listener cold,
As he thought of the stake in that fiery fray,
    With Sheridan twenty miles away.

But there is a road from Winchester town,
A good, broad highway leading down;
And there, through the flush of the morning light,
A steed as black as the steeds of night
Was seen to pass, as with eagle flight;
As if he knew the terrible need,
He stretched away with his utmost speed;
Hills rose and fell; but his heart was gay,
    With Sheridan fifteen miles away.

Still sprung from those swift hoofs, thundering South,
The dust, like smoke from the cannon's mouth;
Or the trail of a comet, sweeping faster and faster.
Foreboding to traitors the doom of disaster,
The heart of the steed and the heart of the master
Were beating like prisoners assaulting their walls,
Impatient to be where the battlefield calls;

35

Every nerve of the charger was strained to full play,
    With Sheridan only ten miles away.

Under his spurning feet the road
Like an arrowy Alpine river flowed,
And the landscape sped away behind
Like an ocean flying before the wind,
And the steed, like a barque fed with furnace ire,
Swept on, with his wild eye full of fire.
But lo! he is nearing his heart's desire;
He is snuffing the smoke of the roaring fray,
    With Sheridan only five miles away.

The first that the general saw were the groups
Of stragglers, and then the retreating troops;
What was done? What to do? A glance told him both,
Then, striking his spurs, with a terrible oath,
He dashed down the line 'mid a storm of huzzas,
And the wave of retreat checked its course there, because
The sight of the master compelled it to pause.
With foam and with dust the black charger was gray;
By the flash of his eye, and the red nostril's play,
He seemed to the whole great army to say,
"I have brought you Sheridan all the way
    From Winchester down to save the day!"

Hurrah! Hurrah for Sheridan!
Hurrah! Hurrah for horse and man!
And when their statues are placed on high,
Under the dome of the Union sky,
The American soldier's Temple of Fame;
There with the glorious general's name,
Be it said, in letters both bold and bright,
    "Here is the steed that saved the day,
By carrying Sheridan into the fight,
    From Winchester, twenty miles away!"

Courtesy J. B. Lippincott Company.

Bettmann

The Present Crisis

JAMES RUSSELL LOWELL
(Born February 22, 1819; died August 12, 1891)

When a deed is done for Freedom, through the broad earth's aching
    breast
Runs a thrill of joy prophetic, trembling on from east to west,
And the slave, where'er he cowers, feels the soul within him climb
To the awful verge of manhood, as the energy sublime
Of the century bursts full-blossomed on the thorny stem of Time.

Through the walls of hut and palace shoots the instantaneous throe,
When the travail of the Ages wrings earth's systems to and fro;
At the birth of each new Era, with a recognizing start,
Nation wildly looks at nation, standing with mute lips apart,
And glad Truth's yet mightier man-child leaps beneath the Future's
    heart.

So the Evil's triumph sendeth, with a terror and a chill,
Under continent to continent, the sense of coming ill,
And the slave, where'er he cowers, feels his sympathies with God
In hot tear-drops ebbing earthward, to be drunk up by the sod,
Till a corpse crawls round unburied, delving in the nobler clod.

For mankind are one in spirit, and an instinct bears along,
Round the earth's electric circle, the swift flash of right or wrong;
Whether conscious or unconscious, yet Humanity's vast frame
Though its ocean-sundered fibres feels the gush of joy or shame;—
In the gain or loss of one race all the rest have equal claim.

Once to every man and nation comes the moment to decide;
In the strife of Truth with Falsehood, for the good or evil side;
Some great cause, God's new Messiah, offering each the bloom or
    blight,
Parts the goats upon the left hand and the sheep upon the right,
And the choice goes by forever 'twixt that darkness and that light.

Hast thou chosen, O my people, on whose party thou shalt stand,
Ere the Doom from its worn sandals shakes the dust against our
   land?
Though the cause of Evil prosper, yet 'tis Truth alone is strong,
And, albeit she wander outcast now, I see around her throng
Troops of beautiful, tall angels, to enshield her from all wrong.

Backward look across the ages and the beacon-moments see,
That, like peaks of some sunk continent, jut through Oblivion's sea;
Not an ear in court or market for the low foreboding cry
Of those Crises, God's stern winnowers, from whose feet earth's
   chaff must fly;
Never shows the choice momentous till the judgment hath passed
   by.

Careless seems the great Avenger; history's page but record
One death-grapple in the darkness 'twixt old systems and the Word;
Truth forever on the scaffold, Wrong forever on the throne,—
Yet that scaffold sways the future, and, behind the dim unknown,
Standeth God within the shadow, keeping watch above his own.

We see dimly in the Present what is small and what is great,
Slow of faith how weak an arm may turn the iron helm of fate,
But the soul is still oracular; amid the market's din,
List the ominous stern whisper from the Delphic cave within,—
"They enslave their children's children who make compromise with
   sin."

Slavery, the earth-born Cyclops, fellest of the giant brood,
Sons of brutish Force and Darkness, who have drenched the earth
   with blood,
Famished in his self-made desert, blinded by our purer day,
Gropes in yet unblasted regions for his miserable prey;
Shall we guide his gory fingers where our helpless children play?

Then to side with Truth is noble when we share her wretched crust,
Ere her cause bring fame and profit, and 'tis prosperous to be just;
Then it is the brave man chooses, while the coward stands aside,
Doubting in his abject spirit, till his Lord is crucified,
And the multitude make virtue of the faith they had denied.

Count me o'er earth's chosen heroes,—they were souls that stood
    alone,
While the men they agonized for hurled the contumelious stone,
Stood serene, and down the future saw the golden beam incline
To the side of perfect justice, mastered by their faith divine,
By one man's plain truth to manhood and to God's supreme design.

By the light of burning heretics Christ's bleeding feet I track,
Toiling up new Calvaries ever with the cross that turns not back,
And these mounts of anguish number how each generation learned
One new word of that grand *Credo* which in prophet-hearts hath
    burned
Since the first man stood God-conquered with his face to heaven
    upturned.

For humanity sweeps onward: where today the martyr stands,
On the morrow crouches Judas with the silver in his hands;
Far in front the cross stands ready and the crackling fagots burn,
While the hooting mob of yesterday in silent awe return
To glean up the scattered ashes into History's golden urn.

'Tis as easy to be heroes as to sit the idle slaves
Of a legendary virtue carved upon our father's graves,
Worshippers of light ancestral make the present light a crime;
Was the Mayflower launched by cowards, steered by men behind
    their time?
Turn those tracks toward Past or Future, that make Plymouth Rock
    sublime?

They were men of present valor, stalwart old iconoclasts,
Unconvinced by axe or gibbet that all virtue was the Past's;
But we make their truth our falsehood thinking that hath made us
    free,
Hoarding it in mouldy parchments, while our tender spirits flee
The rude grasp of that great Impulse which drove them across the
    sea.

They have rights who dare maintain them; we are traitors to our
    sires,
Smothering in their holy ashes Freedom's new-lit altar-fires;

Shall we make their creed our jailor? Shall we, in our haste to slay,
From the tombs of the old prophets steal the funeral lamps away
To light up the martyr-fagots round the prophets of today?

New occasions teach new duties; Time makes ancient good uncouth;
They must upward still, and onward, who would keep abreast of
    Truth;
Lo, before us gleam her camp-fires! we ourselves must Pilgrims be,
Launch our Mayflower, and steer boldly through the desperate
    winter sea,
Nor attempt the Future's portal with the Past's blood-rusted key.

Be Strong

MALTBIE DAVENPORT BABCOCK
(Born August 3, 1858; died May 18, 1901)

Photographed from portrait hanging in the
lecture room of the Brick Presbyterian
Church, New York, of which Dr. Babcock
was formerly pastor.

Be strong!
We are not here to play, to dream, to drift;
We have hard work to do, and loads to lift;
Shun not the struggle—face it; 'tis God's gift.

Be strong!
Say not, "The days are evil. Who's to blame?"
And fold the hands and acquiesce—oh shame!
Stand up, speak out, and bravely, in God's name.

Be strong!
It matters not how deep intrenched the wrong,
How hard the battle goes, the day how long;
Faint not—fight on! To-morrow comes the song.

Columbus

CINCINNATUS HINER MILLER
(known as Joaquin Miller)
*(Born November 10, 1841;
died February, 17, 1913)*

Bettmann
Copyright 1908
J. E. Purdy, Boston

Behind him lay the gray Azores,
   Behind the Gates of Hercules;
Before him not the ghost of shores,
   Before him only shoreless seas.
The good mate said: "Now must we pray,
   For lo! the very stars are gone.
Brave Adm'r'l, speak; what shall I say?"
     "Why, say: 'Sail on! sail on! and on!' "

"My men grow mutinous day by day;
   My men grow ghastly wan and weak."
The stout mate thought of home; a spray
   Of salt wave washed his swarthy cheek.
"What shall I say, brave Adm'r'l, say,
   If we sight naught but seas at dawn?"
"Why, you shall say, at break of day:
   'Sail on! sail on! sail on! and on!' "

They sailed and sailed, as winds might blow,
   Until at last the blanched mate said:
"Why, now not even God would know
   Should I and all my men fall dead.
These very winds forget their way,
   For God from these dread seas is gone.
Now speak, brave Adm'r'l; speak and say"—
   He said: "Sail on! sail on! and on!"

They sailed. They sailed. Then spake the mate:
   "This mad sea shows his teeth to-night;
He curls his lips, he lies in wait,
   With lifted teeth, as if to bite;

41

Brave Adm'r'l, say but one good word;
  What shall we do when hope is gone?"
The words leapt like a leaping sword:
  "Sail on! sail on! sail on! and on!"

Then, pale and worn, he kept his deck,
  And peered through darkness. Ah, that night
Of all dark nights! And then a speck—
  A light! a light! a light! a light!
It grew, a starlit flag unfurled!
  It grew to be Time's burst of dawn.
He gained a world; he gave that world
  Its grandest lesson: "On! sail on!"

From *Complete Poetical Works of Joaquin Miller*. By permission of Whitaker & Ray-Wiggin Co. Copyrighted.

Mercy

From "The Merchant of Venice"

WILLIAM SHAKESPEARE
(Born April 23[?], 1564; died April 23, 1616)

The quality of mercy is not strained;
It droppeth as the gentle rain from heaven
Upon the place beneath: it is twice blest,—
It blesseth him that gives and him that takes:
'Tis mightiest in the mightiest; it becomes
The thronèd monarch better than his crown:
His sceptre shows the force of temporal power,
The attribute to awe and majesty,
Wherein doth sit the dread and fear of kings;
But mercy is above this sceptred sway,—
It is enthronèd in the hearts of kings,
It is an attribute to God himself;
And earthly power doth then show likest God's,
When mercy seasons justice.

Trees

SERGEANT JOYCE KILMER
165th Infantry (69th New York), A.E.F.
*(Born December 6, 1886; killed in action near
Ourcy, July 30, 1918)*

I think that I shall never see
A poem lovely as a tree.

A tree whose hungry mouth is prest
Against the earth's sweet flowing breast;

A tree that looks at God all day,
And lifts her leafy arms to pray;

A tree that may in Summer wear
A nest of robins in her hair;

Upon whose bosom snow has lain;
Who intimately lives with rain.

Poems are made by fools like me,
But only God can make a tree.

Reprinted from *Trees and Other Poems*, by
Joyce Kilmer, by permission of George H.
Doran Company, publishers. Copyright 1914.

The Spires of Oxford
(As seen from the train)

WINIFRED M. LETTS

I saw the spires of Oxford
  As I was passing by,
The grey spires of Oxford
  Against a pearl-grey sky;
My heart was with the Oxford men
  Who went abroad to die.

The years go fast in Oxford,
  The golden years and gay;
The hoary colleges look down
  On careless boys at play,
But when the bugles sounded—War!
  They put their games away.

They left the peaceful river,
  The cricket field, the quad,
The shaven lawns of Oxford,
  To seek a bloody sod.
They gave their merry youth away
  For country and for God.

God rest you, happy gentlemen,
  Who laid your good lives down,
Who took the khaki and the gun
  Instead of cap and gown.
God bring you to a fairer place
  Than even Oxford town.

By permission from *The Spires of Oxford and Other Poems,* by W. M. Letts. Published by E. P. Dutton & Company.

Bettmann

Recessional

RUDYARD KIPLING

(Born December 30, 1865; died January 17, 1936)

God of our fathers, known of old—
   Lord of our far-flung battle line—
Beneath whose awful hand we hold
   Dominion over palm and pine—
Lord God of Hosts, be with us yet,
Lest we forget—lest we forget!

The tumult and the shouting dies—
   The Captains and the Kings depart—
Still stands Thine ancient sacrifice,
   An humble and a contrite heart.
Lord God of Hosts, be with us yet,
Lest we forget—lest we forget!

Far-called, our navies melt away—
   On dune and headland sinks the fire—
Lo, all our pomp of yesterday
   Is one with Nineveh and Tyre!
Judge of the Nations, spare us yet,
Lest we forget—lest we forget!

If, drunk with sight of power, we loose
   Wild tongues that have not Thee in awe—
Such boasting as the Gentiles use,
   Or lesser breeds without the Law—
Lord God of Hosts, be with us yet,
Lest we forget—lest we forget!

For heathen heart that puts her trust
   In reeking tube and iron shard—
All valiant dust that builds on dust,
   And guarding, calls not Thee to guard,
For frantic boast and foolish word,
Thy Mercy on Thy People, Lord! Amen!

Bettmann

The Cloud

PERCY BYSSHE SHELLEY
(Born August 4, 1792; died July 8, 1822)

I bring fresh showers for the thirsting flowers,
　　From the seas and the streams;
I bear light shade for the leaves when laid
　　In their noonday dreams.
From my wings are shaken the dews that waken
　　The sweet buds every one,
When rocked to rest on their mother's breast,
　　As she dances about the sun.
I wield the flail of the lashing hail,
　　And whiten the green plains under,
And then again I dissolve it in rain,
　　And laugh as I pass in thunder.

I sift the snow on the mountains below,
　　And their great pines groan aghast;
And all the night 'tis my pillow white,
　　While I sleep in the arms of the blast.
Sublime on the towers of my skiey bowers,
　　Lightning my pilot sits;
In a cavern under is fettered the thunder,
　　It struggles and howls at fits;
Over earth and ocean, with gentle motion,
　　This pilot is guiding me,
Lured by the love of the genii that move
　　In the depths of the purple sea;
Over the rills, and the crags, and the hills,
　　Over the lakes and the plains,
Wherever he dream, under mountain or stream,
　　The Spirit he loves remains;
And I all the while bask in Heaven's blue smile,
　　Whilst he is dissolving in rains.

The sanguine Sunrise, with his meteor eyes,
    And his burning plumes outspread,
Leaps on the back of my sailing rack,
    When the morning star shines dead;
As on the jag of a mountain crag,
    Which an earthquake rocks and swings,
An eagle alit one moment may sit
    In the light of its golden wings.
And when Sunset may breathe, from the lit sea beneath,
    Its ardours of rest and love,
And the crimson pall of eve may fall
    From the depth of heaven above,
With wings folded I rest, on mine aëry nest,
    As still as a brooding dove.

That orbèd maiden with white fire laden,
    Whom mortals call the Moon,
Glides glimmering o'er my fleece-like floor,
    By the midnight breezes strewn;
And wherever the beat of her unseen feet,
    Which only the angels hear,
May have broken the woof of my tent's thin roof,
    The stars peep behind her and peer;
And I laugh to see them whirl and flee,
    Like a swarm of golden bees,
When I widen the rent in my wind-built tent,
    Till the calm rivers, lakes, and seas,
Like strips of the sky fallen through me on high,
    Are each paved with the moon and these.

I bind the Sun's throne with a burning zone,
    And the Moon's with a girdle of pearl;
The volcanoes are dim, and the stars reel and swim,
    When the whirlwinds my banner unfurl.
From cape to cape, with a bridge-like shape,
    Over a torrent sea,
Sunbeam-proof, I hang like a roof,—
    The mountains its columns be.
The triumphal arch through which I march
    With hurricane, fire, and snow,
When the Powers of the air are chained to my chair,
    Is the million-colored bow;
The sphere-fire above its soft colours wove,
    While the moist Earth was laughing below.

I am the daughter of Earth and Water,
    And the nursling of the Sky;
I pass through the pores of the ocean and shores;
    I change, but I cannot die.
For after the rain when with never a stain
    The pavilion of Heaven is bare,
And the winds and sunbeams with their convex gleams
    Build up the blue dome of air,
I silently laugh at my own cenotaph,
    And out of the caverns of rain,
Like a child from the womb, like a ghost from the tomb,
    I arise and unbuild it again.

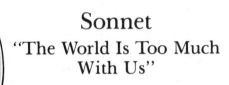

Sonnet
"The World Is Too Much With Us"

WILLIAM WORDSWORTH
(Born April 7, 1770; died April 23, 1850)

Bettmann

The World is too much with us; late and soon,
Getting and spending, we lay waste our powers;
Little we see in Nature that is ours;
We have given our hearts away, a sordid boon!
This sea that bares her bosom to the moon;
The winds that will be howling at all hours,
And are up-gathered now like sleeping flowers;
For this, for everything, we are out of tune;
It moves us not.—Great God! I'd rather be
A Pagan suckled in a creed outworn,
So might I, standing on this pleasant lea,
Have glimpses that would make me less forlorn;
Have sight of Proteus rising from the sea,
Or hear old Triton blow his wreathed horn.

How Did You Die?

EDMUND VANCE COOKE

(Born June 5, 1866; died December 18, 1932)

Did you tackle that trouble that came your way
  With a resolute heart and cheerful?
Or hide your face from the light of day
  With a craven soul and fearful?
Oh, a trouble's a ton, or a trouble's an ounce,
  Or a trouble is what you make it.
And it isn't the fact that you're hurt that counts,
  But only how did you take it?

You are beaten to earth? Well, well, what's that?
  Come up with a smiling face.
It's nothing against you to fall down flat,
  But to lie there—that's disgrace.
The harder you're thrown, why the higher you bounce;
  Be proud of your blackened eye!
It isn't the fact that you're licked that counts;
  It's how did you fight and why?

And though you be done to death, what then?
  If you battled the best you could;
If you played your part in the world of men,
  Why, the Critic will call it good.
Death comes with a crawl, or comes with a pounce,
  And whether he's slow or spry,
It isn't the fact that you're dead that counts,
  But only, how did you die?

Wolsey's Farewell to His Greatness

From "Henry VIII"

JOHN FLETCHER
*(Born December 20, 1579;
died August 28[?], 1625)*

Bettmann
From a portrait in possession of the Earl of
Clarendon (Courtesy *The Outlook*)

Farewell! a long farewell to all my greatness!
This is the state of man: today he puts forth
The tender leaves of hope, to-morrow blossoms,
And bears his blushing honors thick upon him;
The third day comes a frost, a killing frost;
And—when he thinks, good easy man, full surely
His greatness is a-ripening—nips his root,
And then he falls, as I do. I have ventur'd,
Like little wanton boys that swim on bladders,
This many summers in a sea of glory,
But far beyond my depth; my high blown pride
At length broke under me, and now has left me,
Weary and old with service, to the mercy
Of a rude stream, that must forever hide me.
Vain pomp and glory of this world, I hate ye!
I feel my heart new-opened. Oh! how wretched
Is that poor man that hangs on princes' favors!
There is, betwixt that smile we would aspire to,
That sweet aspect of princes, and their ruin,
More pangs and fears than wars or women have;
And when he falls, he falls like Lucifer,
Never to hope again.

This soliloquy of Wolsey occurs in the latter
half of Act 3, Scene 2, of "Henry VIII," a play
now agreed to be in some sense the joint work
of Shakespeare and Fletcher. The soliloquy is
generally accepted as Fletcher's writing.

The Blessed Damozel

DANTE GABRIEL ROSSETTI
(Born May 12, 1828; died April 9, 1882)

Bettmann

The blessed damozel leaned out
  From the gold bar of Heaven;
Her eyes were deeper than the depth
  Of waters stilled at even;
She had three lilies in her hand,
  And the stars in her hair were seven.

Her robe, ungirt from clasp to hem,
  No wrought flowers did adorn,
But a white rose of Mary's gift,
  For service meetly worn;
Her hair that lay along her back
  Was yellow like ripe corn.

Herseemed she scarce had been a day
  One of God's choristers;
The wonder was not yet quite gone
  From that still look of hers;
Albeit, to them she left, her day
  had counted as ten years.

(To one, it is ten years of years.
  . . . Yet now, and in this place,
Surely she leaned o'er me—her hair
  Fell all about my face. . . .
Nothing: the autumn-fall of leaves.
  The whole year sets apace.)

It was the rampart of God's house
  That she was standing on;
By God built over the sheer depth
  The which is Space begun;
So high, that looking downward thence
  She scarce could see the sun.

It lies in Heaven, across the flood
   Of ether, as a bridge.
Beneath, the tides of day and night
   With flame and darkness ridge
The void, as low as where this earth
   Spins like a fretful midge.

Around her, lovers, newly met
   'Mid deathless love's acclaims,
Spake evermore among themselves
   Their heart-remembered names;
And the souls mounting up to God
   Went by her like thin flames.

And still she bowed herself and stooped
   Out of the circling charm;
Until her bosom must have made
   The bar she leaned on warm,
And the lilies lay as if asleep
   Along her bended arm.

From the fixed place of Heaven she saw
   Time like a pulse shake fierce
Through all the worlds. Her gaze still strove
   Within the gulf to pierce
Its path; and now she spoke as when
   The stars sang in their spheres.

The sun was gone now; the curled moon
   Was like a little feather
Fluttering far down the gulf; and now
   She spoke through the still weather.
Her voice was like the voice the stars
   Had when they sang together.

(Ah sweet! Even now, in that bird's song,
   Strove not her accents there,
Fain to be hearkened? When those bells
   Possessed the mid-day air,
Strove not her steps to reach my side
   Down all the echoing stair?)

'I wish that he were come to me,
   For he will come,' she said.
'Have I not prayed in Heaven?—on Earth,

Lord, Lord, has he not pray'd?
   Are not two prayers a perfect strength?
     And shall I feel afraid?

'When round his head the aureole clings,
     And he is clothed in white,
I'll take his hand and go with him
     To the deep wells of light;
As unto a stream we will step down,
     And bathe there in God's sight.

'We two will stand beside that shrine,
     Occult, withheld, untrod,
Whose lamps are stirred continually
     With prayer sent up to God;
And see our old prayers, granted, melt
     Each like a little cloud.

'We two will lie i' the shadow of
     That living mystic tree
Within whose secret growth the Dove
     Is sometimes felt to be,
While every leaf that His plumes touch
     Saith His Name audibly.

'And I myself will teach to him,
     I myself, lying so,
The songs I sing here; which his voice
     Shall pause in, hushed and slow,
And find some knowledge at each pause,
     Or some new thing to know.'

(Alas! We two, we two, thou say'st!
     Yea, one wast thou with me
That once of old. But shall God lift
     To endless unity
The soul whose likeness with thy soul
     Was but its love for thee?)

'We two,' she said, 'will seek the groves
     Where the lady Mary is,
With her five handmaidens, whose names
     Are five sweet symphonies,
Cecily, Gertrude, Magdalen,
     Margaret and Rosalys.

'Circlewise sit they, with bound locks
   And foreheads garlanded;
Into the fine cloth white like flame
   Weaving the golden thread,
To fashion the birth-robes for them
   Who are just born, being dead.

'He shall fear, haply, and be dumb:
   Then will I lay my cheek
To his, and tell about our love,
   Not once abashed or weak:
And the dear Mother will approve
   My pride, and let me speak.

'Herself shall bring us, hand in hand,
   To Him round whom all souls
Kneel, the clear-ranged unnumbered heads
   Bowed with their aureoles:
And angels meeting us shall sing
   To their citherns and citoles.

'There will I ask of Christ the Lord
   Thus much for him and me:—
Only to live as once on earth
   With Love,—only to be,
As then awhile, for ever now
   Together, I and he.'

She gazed and listened and then said,
   Less sad of speech than mild,—
'All this is when he comes.' She ceased.
   The light thrilled towards her, fill'd
With angels in strong level flight.
   Her eyes prayed, and she smil'd.

(I saw her smile.) But soon their path
   Was vague in distant spheres:
And then she cast her arms along
   The golden barriers,
And laid her face between her hands,
   And wept. (I heard her tears.)

America for Me

HENRY VAN DYKE
(Born November 10, 1852; died April 10, 1933)

Bettmann
Copyright J. E. Purdy, Boston

'Tis fine to see the Old World, and travel up and down
Among the famous palaces and cities of renown,
To admire the crumbly castles and the statues of the kings,—
But now I think I've had enough of antiquated things.

So it's home again, and home again, America for me!
My heart is turning home again, and there I long to be,
In the land of youth and freedom beyond the ocean bars,
Where the air is full of sunlight and the flag is full of stars.

Oh, London is a man's town, there's power in the air;
And Paris is a woman's town, with flowers in her hair;
And it's sweet to dream in Venice, and it's great to study Rome;
But when it comes to living there is no place like home.

I like the German fir-woods, in green battalions drilled;
I like the gardens of Versailles with flashing fountains filled;
But, oh, to take your hand, my dear, and ramble for a day
In the friendly western woodland where Nature has her way!

I know that Europe's wonderful, yet something seems to lack:
The Past is too much with her, and the people looking back.
But the glory of the Present is to make the Future free,—
We love our land for what she is and what she is to be.

Oh, it's home again, and home again, America for me!
I want a ship that's westward bound to plough the rolling sea,
To the blessed Land of Room Enough beyond the ocean bars,
Where the air is full of sunlight and the flag is full of stars.

The Gods of the Copybook Headings

RUDYARD KIPLING

(Born December 30, 1865; died January 17, 1936)

As I pass through my incarnations in every age and race,
I make my proper prostrations to the Gods of the Market-Place.
Peering through reverent fingers I watch them flourish and fall,
And the Gods of the Copybook Headings, I notice, outlast them all.

We were living in trees when they met us. They showed us each in
turn
That Water would certainly wet us, as Fire would certainly burn:
But we found them lacking in Uplift, Vision and Breadth of Mind,
So we left them to teach the Gorillas while we followed the March of
Mankind.

We moved as the Spirit listed. *They* never altered their pace,
Being neither cloud nor wind-borne like the Gods of the Market-
Place;
But they always caught up with our progress, and presently word
would come
That a tribe had been wiped off its icefield, or the lights had gone
out in Rome.

With the Hopes that our World is built on they were utterly out of
touch.
They denied that the Moon was Stilton; they denied she was even
Dutch.
They denied that Wishes were Horses; they denied that a Pig had
wings.
So we worshipped the Gods of the Market Who promised these
beautiful things.

When the Cambrian measures were forming, They promised perpet-
ual peace.
They swore, if we gave them our weapons, that the wars of the tribes
would cease.
But when we disarmed They sold us and delivered us bound to our
foe,
And the Gods of the Copybook Headings said: *"Stick to the Devil
you know."*

On the first Feminian Sandstones we were promised the Fuller
Life
(Which started by loving our neighbour and ended by loving his
wife)
Till our women had no more children and the men lost reason and
faith.
And the Gods of the Copybook Headings said: *"The Wages of Sin is
Death."*

In the Carboniferous Epoch we were promised abundance for all,
By robbing selected Peter to pay for collective Paul;
But, though we had plenty of money, there was nothing our money
could buy,
And the Gods of the Copybook Headings said: *"If you don't work
you die."*

Then the Gods of the Market tumbled, and their smooth-tongued
wizards withdrew,
And the hearts of the meanest were humbled and began to believe it
was true
That All is not Gold that Glitters, and Two and Two make Four—
And the Gods of the Copybook Headings limped up to explain it
once more.

       *   *   *   *   *

As it will be in the future, it was at the birth of Man—
There are only four things certain since Social Progress began—
That the Dog returns to his Vomit and the Sow returns to her Mire,
And the burnt Fool's bandaged finger goes wabbling back to the
Fire;
And that after this is accomplished, and the brave new world begins
When all men are paid for existing and no man must pay for his
sins,
As surely as Water will wet us, as surely as Fire will burn,
The Gods of the Copybook Headings with terror and slaughter
return!

Abraham Lincoln Walks at Midnight
In Springfield, Illinois

VACHEL LINDSAY
*(Born Springfield, Ill., November 10, 1879;
died December 5, 1931)*

Bettmann

It is portentous, and a thing of state
That here at midnight, in our little town
A mourning figure walks, and will not rest,
Near the old court-house pacing up and down,
Or by his homestead, or in shadowed yards
He lingers where his children used to play,
Or through the market, on the well-worn stones
He stalks until the dawn-stars burn away.

A bronzed, lank man! His suit of ancient black,
A famous high top-hat and plain worn shawl
Make him the quaint great figure that men love,
The prairie-lawyer, master of us all.

He cannot sleep upon his hillside now.
He is among us:—as in times before!
And we who toss and lie awake for long
Breathe deep, and start, to see him pass the door.

His head is bowed. He thinks on men and kings.
Yea, when the sick world cries, how can he sleep?
Too many peasants fight, they know not why,
Too many homesteads in black terror weep.

The sins of all the war-lords burn his heart.
He sees the dreadnaughts scouring every main.
He carries on his shawl-wrapped shoulders now
The bitterness, the folly and the pain.

He cannot rest until a spirit-dawn
Shall come;—the shining hope of Europe free:
The league of sober folk, the Workers' Earth,
Bringing long peace to Cornland, Alp and Sea.

It breaks his heart that kings must murder still,
That all his hours of travail here for men
Seem yet in vain. And who will bring white peace
That he may sleep upon his hill again?

From *The Congo and Other Poems* by Vachel
Lindsay and published by the Macmillan
Company. Copyright 1914. By special permis-
sion of the author and publisher.

Bettmann

The Man with the Hoe

Written after seeing Millet's world-famous painting of a brutalized toiler

EDWIN MARKHAM

*(Born Oregon City, Oregon, 1852;
died March 7, 1940)*

God made man in his own image,
in the image of God made He him.
—*Genesis*

Bowed by the weight of centuries he leans
Upon his hoe and gazes on the ground,
The emptiness of ages in his face,
And on his back the burden of the world.
Who made him dead to rapture and despair,
A thing that grieves not and that never hopes,
Stolid and stunned, a brother to the ox?
Who loosened and let down this brutal jaw?
Whose was the hand that slanted back this brow?
Whose breath blew out the light within this brain?

Is this the Thing the Lord God made and gave
To have dominion over sea and land;
To trace the stars and search the heavens for power;
To feel the passion of Eternity?
Is this the dream He dreamed who shaped the suns
And markt their ways upon the ancient deep?
Down all the caverns of Hell to their last gulf
There is no shape more terrible than this—
More tongued with censure of the world's blind greed—
More filled with signs and portents for the soul—
More packt with danger to the universe.

What gulfs between him and the seraphim!
Slave of the wheel of labor, what to him
Are Plato and the swing of Pleiades?
What the long reaches of the peaks of song,
The rift of dawn, the reddening of the rose?
Thru this dread shape the suffering ages look;
Time's tragedy is in that aching stoop;
Thru this dread shape humanity betrayed,
Plundered, profaned and disinherited,
Cries protest to the Judges of the World,
A protest that is also prophecy.

O masters, lords and rulers in all lands,
Is this the handiwork you give to God,
This monstrous thing distorted and soul-quencht?
How will you ever straighten up this shape;
Touch it again with immortality;
Give back the upward looking and the light;
Rebuild in it the music and the dream;
Make right the immemorial infamies,
Perfidious wrongs, immedicable woes?

O masters, lords and rulers in all lands,
How will the future reckon with this Man?
How answer his brute question in that hour
When whirlwinds of rebellion shake all shores?
How will it be with kingdoms and with kings—
With those who shaped him to the thing he is—
When this dumb Terror shall rise to judge the world,
After the silence of the centuries?

This poem has been called "The battle-cry of
the next thousand years." It has been trans-
lated into thirty languages. From *The Man
with the Hoe, and Other Poems*, by Edwin
Markham. Published by Doubleday, Page &
Co. Copyright 1899, by the author, and used by
his permission.

Bettmann

The Duel

EUGENE FIELD

*(Born September 3, 1850;
died November 4, 1895)*

The gingham dog and the calico cat
Side by side on the table sat;
'Twas half-past twelve, and (what do you think!)
Nor one nor t' other had slept a wink!
    The old Dutch clock and the Chinese plate
    Appeared to know as sure as fate
There was going to be a terrible spat.

    *(I wasn't there; I simply state
    What was told to me by the Chinese plate!)*

The gingham dog went "bow-wow-wow!"
And the calico cat replied "mee-ow!"
The air was littered, an hour or so,
With bits of gingham and calico,
    While the old Dutch clock in the chimney-place
    Up with its hands before its face,
For it always dreaded a family row!

    *(Never mind: I'm only telling you
    What the old Dutch clock declares is true!)*

The Chinese plate looked very blue,
And wailed, "Oh, dear! what shall we do!"
But the gingham dog and the calico cat
Wallowed this way and tumbled that,
    Employing every tooth and claw
    In the awfullest way you ever saw—
And, oh! how the gingham and calico flew!

    *(Don't fancy I exaggerate—
    I got my news from the Chinese plate!)*

61

Next morning where the two had sat
They found no trace of dog or cat;
And some folk think unto this day
That burglars stole that pair away!
 But the truth about the cat and pup
 Is this: they ate each other up!
Now what do you really think of that!

(The old Dutch clock it told me so,
And that is how I came to know.)

From *The Poems of Eugene Field.* Copyright
1911, Charles Scribner's Sons.

Bettmann

Song of the Chattahoochee

SIDNEY LANIER

(Born February 3, 1842; died September 7, 1881)

Out of the hills of Habersham,
 Down the valleys of Hall,
I hurry amain to reach the plain,
Run the rapid and leap the fall,
Split at the rock and together again,
Accept my bed, or narrow or wide,
And flee from folly on every side
With a lover's pain to attain the plain
 Far from the hills of Habersham,
 Far from the valleys of Hall.

All down the hills of Habersham,
 All through the valleys of Hall,
The rushes cried *Abide, abide,*
The willful waterweeds held me thrall,
The laving laurel turned my tide,
The ferns and the fondling grass said *Stay,*
The dewberry dipped for to work delay,
And the little reeds sighed *Abide, abide,*
 Here in the hills of Habersham
 Here in the valleys of Hall.

High o'er the hills of Habersham,
   Veiling the valleys of Hall,
The hickory told me manifold
Fair tales of shade, the poplar tall
Wrought me her shadowy self to hold,
The chestnut, the oak, the walnut, the pine,
Overleaning, with flickering meaning and sign,
Said, *Pass not, so cold, these manifold*
   Deep shades of the hills of Habersham,
   These glades in the valleys of Hall.

And oft in the hills of Habersham
   And oft in the valleys of Hall,
The white quartz shone, and the smooth brook-stone
Did bar me of passage with friendly brawl,
And many a luminous jewel lone—
Crystals clear or a-cloud with mist,
Ruby, garnet and amethyst—
Made lures with the lights of streaming stone
   In the clefts of the hills of Habersham,
   In the beds of the valleys of Hall.

But oh, not the hills of Habersham,
   And oh, not the valleys of Hall
Avail: I am fain to water the plain.
Downward the voices of Duty call—
Downward, to toil and be mixed with the main;
The dry fields burn, and the mills are to turn,
And a myriad flowers mortally yearn,
And the lordly main beyond the plain
   Calls o'er the hills of Habersham.
   Calls through the valleys of Hall.

From *Poems of Sidney Lanier*. Copyright 1884 and 1891. Published by Charles Scribner's Sons.

Bettmann

Ode on Intimations of Immortality

From Recollections of Early Childhood

WILLIAM WORDSWORTH
(Born April 7, 1770; died April 23, 1850)

The Child is father of the Man;
And I could wish my days to be
Bound each to each by natural piety.

There was a time when meadow, grove, and stream,
The earth, and every common sight,
　　To me did seem
　　Apparelled in celestial light,
The glory and the freshness of a dream.
It is not now as it hath been of yore;—
　　Turn wheresoe'er I may,
　　By night or day,
The things which I have seen I now can see no more.
　　The Rainbow comes and goes,
　　And lovely is the Rose,
　　The Moon doth with delight
Look round her when the heavens are bare,
　　Waters on a starry night
　　Are beautiful and fair;
　　The sunshine is a glorious birth;
　　But yet I know, wher'er I go,
That there hath past away a glory from the earth.

Now, while the birds thus sing a joyous song,
　　And while the young lambs bound
　　As to the tabor's sound,
To me alone there came a thought of grief:
A timely utterance gave that thought relief,
　　And I again am strong:
The cataracts blow their trumpets from the steep;
Nor more shall grief of mine the season wrong;
I hear the Echoes through the mountains throng,
The Winds come to me from the fields of sleep,
　　And all the earth is gay;
　　Land and sea
Give themselves up to jollity,

And with the heart of May
Doth every Beast keep holiday;—
Thou Child of Joy,
Shout round me, let me hear thy shouts, thou happy
Shepherd-boy!

Ye blessèd Creatures, I have heard the call
Ye to each other make; I see
The heavens laugh with you in your jubilee;
My heart is at your festival,
My head hath its coronal,
The fulness of your bliss, I feel—I feel it all.
Oh evil day! if I were sullen
While Earth herself is adorning
This sweet May-morning,
And the Children are culling
On every side,
In a thousand valleys far and wide,
Fresh flowers; while the sun shines warm,
And the Babe leaps up on his Mother's arm:—
I hear, I hear, with joy I hear!
—But there's a tree, of many, one,
A single Field which I have looked upon,
Both of them speak of something that is gone:
The Pansy at my feet
Doth the same tale repeat:
Whither is fled the visionary gleam?
Where is it now, the glory and the dream?

Our birth is but a sleep and a forgetting:
The Soul that rises with us, our life's Star,
Hath had elsewhere its setting,
And cometh from afar:
Not in entire forgetfulness,
And not in utter nakedness,
But trailing clouds of glory do we come
From God, who is our home:
Heaven lies about us in our infancy!
Shades of the prison-house begin to close
Upon the growing Boy,
But He beholds the light, and whence it flows,
He sees it in his joy;
The Youth, who daily farther from the east
Must travel, still is Nature's Priest,
And by the vision splendid

Is on his way attended;
At length the Man perceives it die away,
And fade into the light of common day.

Earth fills her lap with pleasures of her own;
Yearnings she hath in her own natural kind,
And, even with something of a Mother's mind,
And no unworthy aim,
The homely Nurse doth all she can
To make her Foster-child, her Inmate Man,
Forget the glories he hath known,
And the imperial palace whence he came.

Behold the Child among his new-born blisses,
A six years' Darling of a pigmy size!
See, where 'mid work of his own hand he lies,
Fretted by sallies of his mother's kisses,
With light upon him from his father's eyes!
See, at his feet, some little plan or chart,
Some fragment from his dream of human life,
Shaped by himself with newly-learned art;
A wedding or a festival,
A mourning or a funeral;
And this hath now his heart,
And unto this he frames his song:
Then will he fit his tongue
To dialogues of business, love, or strife;
But it will not be long
Ere this be thrown aside,
And with new joy and pride
The little Actor cons another part;
Filling from time to time his "humorous stage"
With all the Persons, down to palsied Age,
That Life brings with her in her equipage;
As if his whole vocation
Were endless imitation.

Thou, whose exterior semblance doth belie
Thy Soul's immensity;
Thou best Philosopher, who yet dost keep
Thy heritage, thou Eye among the blind,
That, deaf and silent, read'st the eternal deep,
Haunted for ever by the eternal mind,—
Mighty Prophet! Seer blest!
On whom those truths do rest,

Which we are toiling all our lives to find,
In darkness lost, the darkness of the grave;
Thou, over whom thy Immortality
Broods like the Day, a master o'er a Slave,
A presence which is not to be put by;
Thou little Child yet glorious in the might
Of heaven-born freedom on thy being's height,
Why with such earnest pains dost thou provoke
The years to bring the inevitable yoke,
Thus blindly with thy blessedness at strife?
Full soon thy Soul shall have her earthly freight,
And custom lie upon thee with a weight,
Heavy as frost, and deep almost as life!

Oh joy! that in our embers
Is something that doth live,
That nature yet remembers
What was so fugitive!
The thought of our past years in me doth breed
Perpetual benediction: not indeed
For that which is most worthy to be blest;
Delight and liberty, the simple creed
Of Childhood, whether busy or at rest,
With new-fledged hope still fluttering in his breast:—
Not for these I raise
The song of thanks and praise;
But for those obstinate questionings
Of sense and outward things,
Fallings from us, vanishings;
Blank misgivings of a Creature
Moving about in worlds not realised,
High instincts before which our mortal Nature
Did tremble like a guilty Thing surprised:
But for those first affections,
Those shadowy recollections,
Which, be they what they may,
Are yet the fountain-light of all our day,
Are yet a master-light of all our seeing;
Uphold us, cherish, and have power to make
Our noisy years seem moments in the being
Of the eternal Silence: truths that wake,
To perish never:
Which neither listlessness, nor mad endeavour,
Nor Man nor Boy,
Nor all that is at enmity with joy,

Can utterly abolish or destroy!
      Hence in a season of calm weather,
        Though inland far we be,
Our Souls have sight of that immortal sea
        Which brought us hither,
      Can in a moment travel thither,
And see the Children sport upon the shore,
And hear the mighty waters rolling evermore.

Then sing, ye Birds, sing, sing a joyous song!
      And let the young Lambs bound
      As to the tabor's sound!
We in thought will join your throng,
    Ye that pipe and ye that play,
    Ye that through your hearts today
    Feel the gladness of the May!
What though the radiance which was once so bright
Be now for ever taken from my sight,
    Though nothing can bring back the hour
Of splendour in the grass, of glory in the flower;
      We will grieve not, rather find
      Strength in what remains behind;
      In the primal sympathy
      Which having been must ever be;
      In the soothing thoughts that spring
      Out of human suffering;
      In the faith that looks through death,
In years that bring the philosophic mind.

And O, ye Fountains, Meadows, Hills, and Groves,
Forbode not any severing of our loves!
Yet in my heart of hearts I feel your might;
I only have relinquished one delight
To live beneath your more habitual sway.
I love the Brooks which down their channels fret,
Even more than when I tripped lightly as they;
The innocent brightness of a new-born Day
      Is lovely yet;
The Clouds that gather round the setting sun
Do take a sober colouring from an eye
That hath kept watch o'er man's mortality;
Another race hath been, and other palms are won.
Thanks to the human heart by which we live,
Thanks to its tenderness, its joys, and fears,
To me the meanest flower that blows can give
Thoughts that do often lie too deep for tears.

Bettmann

Letter to a Young Friend

ROBERT BURNS

(Born January 25, 1759; died July 21, 1796)

I lang hae thought, my youthfu' friend,
    A something to have sent you,
Tho' it should serve nae ither end
    Than just a kind memento:
But how the subject-theme may gang
    Let time and chance determine:
Perhaps it may turn out a sang;
    Perhaps, turn out a sermon.

Ye'll try the world fu' soon, my lad;
    And, Andrew dear, believe me,
Ye'll find mankind an unco squad,
    And muckle they may grieve ye:
For care and trouble set your thought,
    Ev'n when your end's attainèd:
And a' your views may come to nought,
    Where every nerve is strainèd.

I'll no say, men are villains a':
    The real, harden'd wicked,
Wha hae nae check but human law,
    Are to a few restricked;
But, och! mankind are unco weak
    An' little to be trusted;
If Self the wavering balance shake,
    It's rarely right adjusted!

Yet they what fa' in Fortune's strife,
    Their fate we should na censure;
For still, th' important end of life
    They equally may answer:
A man may hae an honest heart,

Tho' poortith hourly stare him:
A man may tak a neebor's part,
   Yet hae nae cash to spare him.

Ay free, aff han', your story tell,
   When wi' a bosom cronie;
But still keep something to yoursel
   Ye scarcely tell to onie:
Conceal yoursel as weel's ye can
   Frae critical dissection:
But keek thro' every other man
   Wi' sharpen'd, sly inspection.

The sacred lowe o' weell-plac'd love,
   Luxuriantly indulge it;
But never tempt th' illicit rove,
   Tho' naething should divulge it:
I waive the quantum o' the sin,
   The hazard of concealing;
But, och! it hardens a' within,
   And petrifies the feeling!

To catch Dame Fortune's golden smile,
   Assiduous wait upon her;
And gather gear by every wile
   That's justify'd by honour:
Not for to hide it in a hedge,
   Nor for a train-attendant;
But for the glorious privilege
   Of being independent.

The fear o' Hell's a hangman's whip
   To haud the wretch in order;
But where ye feel your honour grip,
   Let that ay be your border:
Its slightest touches, instant pause—
   Debar a' side-pretences;
And resolutely keep its laws,
   Uncaring consequences.

The great Creator to revere
   Must sure become the creature;
But still the preaching cant forbear
   And ev'n the rigid feature:
Yet ne'er with wits profane to range

Be complaisance extended;
An atheist-laugh's a poor exchange
    For Deity offended!

When ranting round in Pleasure's ring,
    Religion may be blinded;
Or if she gie a random sting,
    It may be little minded;
But when on Life we're tempest-driv'n—
    A conscience but a canker—
A correspondence fix'd wi' Heav'n
    Is sure a noble anchor!

Adieu, dear, amiable youth!
    Your heart can ne'er be wanting!
May prudence, fortitude, and truth,
    Erect your brow undaunting!
In ploughman phrase, "God send you speed,"
    Still daily to grow wiser;
And may ye better reck the rede,
    Than ever did th' adviser!

Requiem

ROBERT LOUIS STEVENSON
*(Born November 13, 1850;
died December 3, 1894)*

Under the wide and starry sky
    Dig the grave and let me lie:
Glad did I live and gladly die,
    And I laid me down with a will.

This be the verse you grave for me:
*Here he lies where he long'd to be;
Home is the sailor, home from the sea,
    And the hunter home from the hill.*

71

Bettmann

The Deacon's Masterpiece
or "The One-Hoss Shay"

OLIVER WENDELL HOLMES
(Born August 29, 1809; died October 7, 1894)

Have you heard of the wonderful one-hoss shay,
That was built in such a logical way
It ran a hundred years to a day,
And then, of a sudden, it—ah, but stay,
I'll tell you what happened without delay,
Scaring the parson into fits,
Frightening people out of their wits,—
Have you heard of that, I say?

Seventeen hundred and fifty-five.
Georgius Secundus was then alive,—
Snuffy old drone from the German hive.
That was the year when Lisbon-town
Saw the earth open and gulp her down,
And Braddock's army was done so brown,
Left without a scalp to its crown.
It was on the terrible, Earthquake-day
That the Deacon finished the one-hoss shay.

Now in building of chaises, I tell you what,
There is always *somewhere* a weakest spot,—
In hub, tire, felloe, in spring or thill,
In panel, or crossbar, or floor, or sill,
In screw, bolt, thoroughbrace,—lurking still,
Find it somewhere you must and will,—
Above or below, or within or without,—
And that's the reason, beyond a doubt,
A chaise *breaks down,* but doesn't *wear out.*

But the Deacon swore (as Deacons do,
With an "I dew vum," or an "I tell yeou")
He would build one shay to beat the taown

72

'N the keounty 'n' all the kentry raoun':
It should be so built that it *couldn'* break daown:
"Fur," said the Deacon, "'t's mighty plain
Thut the weakes' places mus' stan' the strain;
'N' the way t' fix it, uz I maintain,
                                        Is only jest
T' make that place uz strong uz the rest."

So the Deacon inquired of the village folk
Where he could find the strongest oak,
That couldn't be split nor bent nor broke,—
That was for spokes and floor and sills;
He sent for lancewood to make the thills;
The crossbars were ash, from the straightest trees;
The panels of white-wood, that cuts like cheese,
But lasts like iron for things like these;
The hubs of logs from the "Settler's ellum,"—
Last of its timber,—they couldn't sell 'em,
Never an axe had seen their chips,
And the wedges flew from between their lips,
Their blunt ends frizzled like celery-tips;
Step and prop-iron, bolt and screw,
Spring, tire, axle, and linchpin too,
Steel of the finest, bright and blue;
Thoroughbrace bison-skin, thick and wide;
Boot, top, dasher, from tough old hide
Found in the pit when the tanner died.
That was the way he "put her through."—
"There!" said the Deacon, "naow she'll dew!"

Do! I tell you, I rather guess
She was a wonder, and nothing less!
Colts grew horses, beards turned gray,
Deacon and deaconess dropped away,
Children and grandchildren—where were they?
But there stood the stout old one-hoss shay
As fresh as on Lisbon-earthquake-day!
EIGHTEEN HUNDRED;—it came and found
The Deacon's masterpiece strong and sound.
Eighteen hundred increased by ten;—
"Hahnsum kerridge" they called it then.
Eighteen hundred and twenty came;—
Running as usual; much, the same.
Thirty and forty at last arrive,
And then come fifty, and FIFTY-FIVE.

Little of all we value here
Wakes on the morn of its hundredth year
Without both feeling and looking queer.
In fact, there's nothing that keeps its youth,
So far as I know, but a tree and truth.
(This is a moral that runs at large;
Take it. You're welcome. No extra charge.)
FIRST OF NOVEMBER,—the Earthquake-day.—
There are traces of age in the one-hoss shay,
A general flavor of mild decay,
But nothing local as one may say.
There couldn't be,—for the Deacon's art
Had made it so like in every part
That there wasn't a chance for one to start.
For the wheels were just as strong as the thills,
And the floor was just as strong as the sills,
And the panels just as strong as the floor,
And the whippletree neither less nor more,
And the back-crossbar as strong as the fore,
And spring and axle and hub *encore.*
And yet, *as a whole,* it is past a doubt
In another hour it will be *worn out!*

First of November, 'Fifty-five!
This morning the parson takes a drive.
Now, small boys, get out of the way!
Here comes the wonderful one-hoss shay,
Drawn by a rat-tailed, ewe-necked bay.
"Huddup!" said the parson. Off went they.
The parson was working his Sunday's text,—
Had got to *fifthly,* and stopped perplexed
At what the—Moses—was coming next.
All at once the horse stood still,
Close by the meet'n'-house on the hill.
—First a shiver, and then a thrill,
Then something decidedly like a spill,—
And the parson was sitting up on a rock,
At half-past nine by the meet'n'-house clock,—
Just the hour of the Earthquake shock!
—What do you think the parson found,
When he got up and stared around?
The poor old chaise in a heap or mound,
As if it had been to the mill and ground!

You see, of course, if you're not a dunce,
How it went to pieces all at once,—
All at once, and nothing first,—
Just as bubbles do when they burst.

End of the wonderful one-hoss shay,
Logic is logic. That's all I say.

Bettmann

The Building of the Ship

HENRY WADSWORTH LONGFELLOW
(Born February 27, 1807; died March 24, 1882)

Then the Master,
With a gesture of command,
Waved his hand;
And at the word,
Loud and sudden there was heard,
All around them and below,
The sound of hammers, blow on blow,
Knocking away the shores and spurs.
And see! she stirs!
She starts—she moves—she seems to feel
The thrill of life along her keel,
And, spurning with her foot the ground,
With one exulting, joyous bound,
She leaps into the ocean's arms!

And lo! from the assembled crowd
There rose a shout, prolonged and loud,
That to the ocean seemed to say,
"Take her, O bridegroom, old and gray,
Take her to thy protecting arms,
With all her youth and all her charms!"

How beautiful she is! How fair
She lies within those arms, that press
Her form with many a soft caress
Of tenderness and watchful care!
Sail forth into the sea, O ship!
Through wind and wave, right onward steer.
The moistened eye, the trembling lip,
And not the signs of doubt or fear.

Sail forth into the sea of life,
O gentle, loving, trusting wife,
And safe from all adversity
Upon the bosom of that sea
Thy comings and thy goings be!
For gentleness and love and trust
Prevail o'er angry wave and gust;
And in the wreck of noble lives
Something immortal still survives!

Thou, too, sail on, O ship of State!
Sail on, O Union, strong and great!
Humanity with all its fears,
With all the hopes of future years,
Is hanging breathless on thy fate!
We know what Master laid thy keel,
What Workman wrought thy ribs of steel,
Who made each mast, and sail, and rope,
What anvils rang, what hammers beat,
In what a forge and what a heat,
Were shaped the anchors of thy hope!
Fear not each sudden sound and shock,
'Tis of the wave and not the rock;
'Tis but the flapping of the sail,
And not a rent made by the gale.
In spite of rock and tempest's roar,
In spite of false lights on the shore,
Sail on, nor fear to breast the sea!
Our hearts, our hopes, are all with thee,
Our hearts, our hopes, our prayers, our tears,
Our faith triumphant o'er our fears,
Are all with thee—are all with thee!

Bettmann

Solitude

ELLA WHEELER WILCOX
(Born November 5, 1855; died October 30, 1919)

Laugh, and the world laughs with you;
   Weep, and you weep alone.
For the sad old earth must borrow its mirth,
   But has trouble enough of its own.
Sing, and the hills will answer;
   Sigh, it is lost on the air.
The echoes bound to a joyful sound,
   But shrink from voicing care.

Rejoice, and men will seek you;
   Grieve, and they turn and go.
They want full measure of all your pleasure,
   But they do not need your woe.
Be glad, and your friends are many;
   Be sad, and you lose them all.
There are none to decline your nectared wine,
   But alone you must drink life's gall.

Feast, and your halls are crowded;
   Fast, and the world goes by.
Succeed and give, and it helps you live,
   But no man can help you die.
There is room in the halls of pleasure
   For a long and lordly train,
But one by one we must all file on
   Through the narrow aisles of pain.

Reprinted from *Poems of Passion* by Ella Wheeler Wilcox. By special permission W. B. Conkey Company, Hammond, Ind.

Photograph by Mecca Studio

Knee-Deep in June

JAMES WHITCOMB RILEY
(Born October 7, 1849; died July 22, 1916)

Tell you what I like the best—
  'Long about knee-deep in June,
'Bout the time strawberries melts
  On the vine,—some afternoon
Like to jes' git out and rest,
  And not work at nothin' else!

Orchard's where I'd ruther be—
Needn't fence it in for me!—
  Jes' the whole sky overhead,
And the whole airth underneath—
Sorto' so's a man kin breathe
  Like he ort, and kindo' has
Elbow room to keerlessly
  Sprawl out len'thways on the grass
    Where the shadders thick and soft
  As the kivvers on the bed
    Mother fixes in the loft
Allus, when they's company!

Jes' a-sorto' lazin' there—
  S'lazy, 'at you peek and peer
    Through the wavin' leaves above,
    Like a feller 'at's in love
  And don't know it, ner don't keer!
Ever'thing you hear and see
    Got some sorto' interest—
    Maybe find a bluebird's nest
  Tucked up there conveenently
  Fer the boy 'at's ap' to be

Up some other apple-tree!
Watch the swallers skootin' past
'Bout as peert as you could ast;
    Er the Bob-white raise and whiz
    Where some other's whistle is.

Ketch a shadder down below,
And look up to find the crow—
Er a hawk—away up there,
'Peerantly froze in the air!—
    Hear the old hen squawk, and squat
    Over ever' chick she's got,
Suddent-like—and she knows where
    That-air hawk is, well as you!—
    You jes' bet yer life she do!—
        Eyes a-glitterin' like glass,
        Waitin' till he makes a pass!

Pee-wees' singin', to express
    My opinion, 's second class,
Yit you'll hear 'em more er less;
        Sapsucks gittin' down to biz,
Weedin' out the lonesomeness;
    Mr. Bluejay, full o' sass,
        In them base-ball clothes o' his,
Sportin' round the orchard jes'
Like he owned the premises!
        Sun out in the fields kin sizz,
But flat on yer back, I guess,
        In the shade 's where glory is!
That's jes' what I'd like to do
Stiddy fer a year er two!

Plague! ef they ain't somepin' in
Work 'at kindo' goes ag'in
    My convictions!—'long about
        Here in June especially!—
        Under some old apple-tree,
            Jes' a-restin' through and through,
    I could git along without
            Nothin' else at all to do
            Only jes' a-wishin' you
            Wuz a-gittin' there like me,
            And June was eternity!

Lay out there and try to see
Jes' how lazy you kin be!—
   Tumble round and souse yer head
     In the clover-bloom, er pull
     Yer straw hat acrost yer eyes
     And peek through it at the skies,
Thinkin' of old chums 'at's dead;
     Maybe smilin' back at you
     I' betwixt the beautiful
     Clouds o' gold and white and blue!—
Month a man kin railly love—
June, you know, I'm talkin' of!

March ain't never nothin' new!—
Aprile's altogether too
   Brash fer me! and May—I jes'
   'Bominate its promises,—
Little hints o' sunshine and
Green around the timber-land—
   A few promises, and a few
   Chip-birds, and a sprout er two,—
     Drap asleep, and it turns in
     'Fore daylight and snows ag'in!—

But when June comes—Clear my throat
   With wild honey!—Rench my hair
In the dew! and hold my coat!
   Whoop out loud! and throw my hat!—
June wants me, and I'm to spare!
Spread them shadders anywhere,
I'll git down and waller there,
   And obleeged to you at that!

From *Afterwhiles,* by James Whitcomb Riley.
Copyright 1898. Used by special permission of
the publishers, The Bobbs-Merrill Company.

Bettmann

Waiting

JOHN BURROUGHS
(Born April 3, 1837; died March 29, 1921)

Serene, I fold my hands and wait,
  Nor care for wind nor tide nor sea;
I rave no more 'gainst time or fate,
  For lo! my own shall come to me.

I stay my haste, I make delays—
  For what avails this eager pace?
I stand amid the eternal ways
  And what is mine shall know my face.

Asleep, awake, by night or day,
  The friends I seek are seeking me,
No wind can drive my bark astray
  Nor change the tide of destiny.

What matter if I stand alone?
  I wait with joy the coming years;
My heart shall reap where it has sown,
  And garner up its fruit of tears.

The waters know their own, and draw
  The brook that springs in yonder height;
So flows the good with equal law
  Unto the soul of pure delight.

The stars come nightly to the sky;
  The tidal wave unto the sea;
Nor time, nor space, nor deep, nor high,
  Can keep my own away from me.

Bettmann

Paul Revere's Ride

HENRY WADSWORTH LONGFELLOW
(Born February 27, 1807; died March 24, 1882)

Listen, my children, and you shall hear
Of the midnight ride of Paul Revere,
On the eighteenth of April, in Seventy-five;
Hardly a man is now alive
Who remembers that famous day and year.

He said to his friend, "If the British march
By land or sea from the town to-night,
Hang a lantern aloft in the belfry arch
Of the North Church tower as a signal light,—
One if by land, and two if by sea;
And I on the opposite shore will be,
Ready to ride and spread the alarm
Through every Middlesex village and farm,
For the country folk to be up and to arm."

Then he said "Good-night!" and with muffled oar
Silently rowed to the Charlestown shore,
Just as the moon rose over the bay,
Where swinging wide at her moorings lay
The *Somerset,* British man-of-war;
A phantom ship, with each mast and spar
Across the moon like a prison bar,
And a huge black hulk, that was magnified
By its own reflection in the tide.

Meanwhile, his friend through alley and street
Wanders and watches, with eager ears,
Till in the silence around him he hears
The muster of men at the barrack door,
The sound of arms, and the tramp of feet,
And the measured tread of the grenadiers,
Marching down to their boats on the shore.

Then he climbed the tower of the Old North Church,
By the wooden stairs, with stealthy tread,
To the belfry chamber overhead,
And startled the pigeons from their perch
On the sombre rafters, that round him made
Masses and moving shapes of shade,—
By the trembling ladder, steep and tall,
To the highest window in the wall,
Where he paused to listen and look down
A moment on the roofs of the town
And the moonlight flowing over all.

Beneath, in the churchyard, lay the dead,
In their night encampment on the hill,
Wrapped in silence so deep and still
That he could hear, like a sentinel's tread,
The watchful night-wind, as it went
Creeping along from tent to tent,
And seeming to whisper, "All is well!"
A moment only he feels the spell
Of the place and the hour, and the secret dread
Of the lonely belfry and the dead;
For suddenly all his thoughts are bent
On a shadowy something far away,
Where the river widens to meet the bay,—
A line of black that bends and floats
On the rising tide like a bridge of boats.

Meanwhile, impatient to mount and ride,
Booted and spurred, with a heavy stride
On the opposite shore walked Paul Revere.
Now he patted his horse's side,
Now he gazed at the landscape far and near,
Then, impetuous, stamped the earth,
And turned and tightened his saddle girth;
But mostly he watched with eager search
The belfry tower of the Old North Church,
As it rose above the graves on the hill,
Lonely and spectral and sombre and still.
And lo! as he looks, on the belfry's height
A glimmer, and then a gleam of light!
He springs to the saddle, the bridle he turns,
But lingers and gazes, till full on his sight
A second lamp in the belfry burns.

A hurry of hoofs in a village street,
A shape in the moonlight, a bulk in the dark,
And beneath, from the pebbles, in passing, a spark
Struck out by a steed flying fearless and fleet;
That was all! And yet, through the gloom and the light,
The fate of a nation was riding that night;
And the spark struck out by that steed, in his flight,
Kindled the land into flame with its heat.
He has left the village and mounted the steep,
And beneath him, tranquil and broad and deep,
Is the Mystic, meeting the ocean tides;
And under the alders that skirt its edge,
Now soft on the sand, now loud on the ledge,
Is heard the tramp of his steed as he rides.

It was twelve by the village clock
When he crossed the bridge into Medford town.
He heard the crowing of the cock,
And the barking of the farmer's dog,
And felt the damp of the river fog,
That rises after the sun goes down.

It was one by the village clock,
When he galloped into Lexington.
He saw the gilded weathercock
Swim in the moonlight as he passed,
And the meeting-house windows, black and bare,
Gaze at him with a spectral glare,
As if they already stood aghast
At the bloody work they would look upon.

It was two by the village clock,
When he came to the bridge in Concord town.
He heard the bleating of the flock,
And the twitter of birds among the trees,
And felt the breath of the morning breeze
Blowing over the meadow brown.
And one was safe and asleep in his bed
Who at the bridge would be first to fall,
Who that day would be lying dead,
Pierced by a British musket ball.

You know the rest. In the books you have read
How the British Regulars fired and fled,—
How the farmers gave them ball for ball,

From behind each fence and farmyard wall,
Chasing the redcoats down the lane,
Then crossing the fields to emerge again
Under the trees at the turn of the road,
And only pausing to fire and load.

So through the night rode Paul Revere;
And so through the night went his cry of alarm
To every Middlesex village and farm,—
A cry of defiance, and not of fear,
A voice in the darkness, a knock at the door,
And a word that shall echo for evermore!
For, borne on the night-wind of the Past,
Through all our history, to the last,
In the hour of darkness and peril and need,
The people will waken and listen to hear
The hurrying hoof-beats of that steed,
And the midnight message of Paul Revere.

Bettmann

Opportunity

JOHN JAMES INGALLS
(Born December 29, 1833; died July 16, 1900)

Master of human destinies am I.
Fame, love, and fortune on my footsteps wait,
Cities and fields I walk; I penetrate
Deserts and seas remote, and, passing by
Hovel, and mart, and palace, soon or late
I knock unbidden, once at every gate!
If sleeping, wake—if feasting, rise before
I turn away. It is the hour of fate,
And they who follow me reach every state
Mortals desire, and conquer every foe
Save death; but those who doubt or hesitate,
Condemned to failure, penury and woe,
Seek me in vain and uselessly implore—
I answer not, and I return no more.

85

Bettmann

Plant a Tree

LUCY LARCOM
(Born, March 5, 1826[?]; died April 27, 1893)

He who plants a tree
  Plants a hope.
  Rootlets up through fibres blindly grope;
Leaves unfold into horizons free.
  So man's life must climb
  From the clods of time
  Unto heavens sublime.
Canst thou prophesy, thou little tree,
What the glory of thy boughs shall be?

He who plants a tree
  Plants a joy;
  Plants a comfort that will never cloy;
Every day a fresh reality,
  Beautiful and strong,
  To whose shelter throng
  Creatures blithe wih song.
If thou couldst but know, thou happy tree,
Of the bliss that shall inhabit thee!

He who plants a tree,—
  He plants peace.
  Under its green curtains jargons cease.
Leaf and zephyr murmur soothingly;
  Shadows soft with sleep
  Down tired eyelids creep,
  Balm of slumber deep.
Never has thou dreamed, thou blessèd tree,
Of the benediction thou shalt be.

He who plants a tree,—
  He plants youth;

Vigor won for centuries in sooth;
Life of time, that hints eternity!
  Boughs their strength uprear:
  New shoots, every year,
  On old growths appear;
Thou shalt teach the ages, sturdy tree,
Youth of soul is immortality.

He who plants a tree,—
  He plants love,
  Tents of coolness spreading out above
Wayfarers he may not live to see.
  Gifts that grow are best;
  Hands that bless are blest;
  Plant! life does the rest!
Heaven and earth help him who plants a tree,
And his work its own reward shall be.

Bettmann

Sonnet On His Blindness

JOHN MILTON
(Born December 9, 1608; died November 8, 1674)

When I consider how my light is spent
  Ere half my days, in this dark world and wide,
  And that one talent, which is death to hide,
Lodged with me useless, though my soul more bent
To serve therewith my Maker, and present
  My true account, lest He, returning, chide:
  "Doth God exact day labor, light denied?"
I fondly ask; but Patience, to prevent
  That murmur, soon replies, "God doth not need
    Either man's work, or His own gifts; who best
Bear His mild yoke, they serve Him best. His state
  Is kingly. Thousands at His bidding speed,
    And post o'er land and ocean without rest;
They also serve who only stand and wait."

Bettmann

The Bells

EDGAR ALLAN POE
(Born January 19, 1809; died October 7, 1849)

Hear the sledges with the bells—
Silver bells!
What a world of merriment their melody foretells!
How they tinkle, tinkle, tinkle,
In the icy air of night!
While the stars that oversprinkle
All the heavens, seem to twinkle
With a crystalline delight;
Keeping time, time, time,
In a sort of Runic rhyme,
To the tintinnabulation that so musically wells
From the bells, bells, bells, bells,
Bells, bells, bells,—
From the jingling and the tinkling of the bells.

Hear the mellow wedding bells,
Golden bells!
What a world of happiness their harmony foretells!
Through the balmy air of night
How they ring out their delight!
From the molten-golden notes,
And all in tune,
What a liquid ditty floats
To the turtle dove that listens, while she gloats
On the moon!
Oh, from out the sounding cells,
What a gush of euphony voluminously wells!
How it swells!
How it dwells
On the Future! how it tells
Of the rapture that impels
To the swinging and the ringing

Of the bells, bells, bells,
Of the bells, bells, bells, bells,
Bells, bells, bells,—
To the rhyming and the chiming of the bells!

Hear the loud alarum bells—
Brazen bells!
What a tale of terror now their turbulency tells!
In the startled ear of night
How they scream out their affright!
Too much horrified to speak
They can only shriek, shriek,
Out of tune,
In a clamorous appealing to the mercy of the fire,
In a mad expostulation with the deaf and frantic fire,
Leaping higher, higher, higher,
With a desperate desire,
And a resolute endeavor,
Now—now to sit or never,
By the side of the pale-faced moon.
Oh, the bells, bells, bells!
What a tale their terror tells
Of despair!
How they clang, and clash, and roar!
What a horror they outpour
On the bosom of the palpitating air!
Yet the ear it fully knows,
By the twanging,
And the clanging,
How the danger ebbs and flows;
Yet the ear distinctly tells,
In the jangling,
And the wrangling,
How the danger sinks and swells,
By the sinking or the swelling in the anger of the bells—
Of the bells—
Of the bells, bells, bells, bells,
Bells, bells, bells,—
In the clamor and the clangor of the bells!

Hear the tolling of the bells—
Iron bells!
What a world of solemn thought their monody compels!
In the silence of the night,
How we shiver with affright

At the melancholy menace of their tone!
  For every sound that floats
  From the rust within their throats
    Is a groan.
  And the people—ah, the people—
  They that dwell up in the steeple,
    All alone,
And who tolling, tolling, tolling,
  In that muffled monotone,
Feel a glory in so rolling
  On the human heart a stone—
They are neither man nor woman—
They are neither brute nor human—
  They are Ghouls:
And their king it is who tolls;
And he rolls, rolls, rolls,
    Rolls
  A paean from the bells!
And his merry bosom swells
  With the paean of the bells!
And he dances, and he yells;
Keeping time, time, time,
In a sort of Runic rhyme,
  To the paean of the bells—
    Of the bells:
  Keeping time, time, time,
In a sort of Runic rhyme,
  To the throbbing of the bells—
      Of the bells, bells, bells—
  To the sobbing of the bells;
Keeping time, time, time,
      As he knells, knells, knells,
In a happy Runic rhyme,
      To the rolling of the bells—
    Of the bells, bells, bells—
      To the tolling of the bells,
    Of the bells, bells, bells, bells—
      Bells, bells, bells—
To the moaning and the groaning of the bells!

Elegy Written in a Country Church-Yard

Thomas Gray
(Born December 26, 1716; died July 30, 1771)

Bettmann
From the picture by John G. Eccardt in the
National Portrait Gallery (Courtesy *The
Academy*)

The Curfew tolls the knell of parting day,
  The lowing herd wind slowly o'er the lea,
The ploughman homeward plods his weary way,
  And leaves the world to darkness and to me.

Now fades the glimmering landscape on the sight,
  And all the air a solemn stillness holds,
Save where the beetle wheels his droning flight,
  And drowsy tinklings lull the distant folds;

Save that, from yonder ivy-mantled tow'r
  The moping owl does to the moon complain
Of such as, wandering near her secret bow'r,
  Molest her ancient solitary reign.

Beneath those rugged elms, that yew-tree's shade.
  Where heaves the turf in many a mould'ring heap,
Each in his narrow cell for ever laid,
  The rude Forefathers of the hamlet sleep.

The breezy call of incense-breathing Morn,
  The swallow twitt'ring from the straw-built shed,
The cock's shrill clarion, or the echoing horn,
  No more shall rouse them from their lowly bed.

For them no more the blazing hearth shall burn,
  Or busy housewife ply her evening care:
No children run to lisp their sire's return,
  Or climb his knees the envied kiss to share.

Oft did the harvest to their sickle yield,
   Their furrow oft the stubborn glebe has broke;
How jocund did they drive their team afield!
   How bow'd the woods beneath their sturdy stroke!

Let not ambition mock their useful toil,
   Their homely joys, and destiny obscure;
Nor Grandeur hear with a disdainful smile,
   The short and simple annals of the poor.

The boast of heraldry, the pomp of pow'r,
   And all that beauty, all that wealth e'er gave,
Awaits alike th' inevitable hour.
   The paths of glory lead but to the grave.

Nor you, ye Proud, impute to These the fault,
   If Mem'ry o'er their Tomb no Trophies raise,
Where thro' the long-drawn isle and fretted vault
   The pealing anthem swells the note of praise.

Can storied urn or animated bust
   Back to its mansion call the fleeting breath?
Can Honour's voice provoke the silent dust,
   Or Flatt'ry soothe the dull cold ear of Death?

Perhaps in this neglected spot is laid
   Some heart once pregnant with celestial fire;
Hands, that the rod of empire might have sway'd,
   Or wak'd to ecstasy the living lyre.

But Knowledge to their eyes her ample page
   Rich the spoils of time did ne'er unroll;
Chill Penury repress'd their noble rage,
   And froze the genial current of the soul.

Full many a gem of purest ray serene,
   The dark, unfathom'd caves of ocean bear:
Full many a flower is born to blush unseen,
   And waste its sweetness on the desert air.

Some village-Hampden, that with dauntless breast
   The little Tyrant of his fields withstood;
Some mute inglorious Milton here may rest,
   Some Cromwell guiltless of his country's blood.

Th' applause of list'ning senates to command,
　The threats of pain and ruin to despise,
To scatter plenty o'er a smiling land,
　And read their hist'ry in a nation's eyes,

Their lot forbad: nor circumscrib'd alone
　Their growing virtues, but their crimes confin'd;
Forbad to wade through slaughter to a throne,
　And shut the gates of mercy on mankind,

The struggling pangs of conscious truth to hide,
　To quench the blushes of ingenuous shame,
Or heap the shrine of Luxury and Pride
　With incense kindled at the Muse's flame.

Far from the madding crowd's ignoble strife,
　Their sober wishes never learned to stray;
Along the cool sequester'd vale of life
　They kept the noiseless tenor of their way.

Yet ev'n these bones from insult to protect,
　Some frail memorial still erected nigh,
With uncouth rhimes and shapeless sculpture deck'd,
　Implores the passing tribute of a sigh.

Their names, their years, spelt by th' unletter'd muse,
　The place of fame and elegy supply:
And many a holy text around she strews,
　That teach the rustic moralist to die.

For who to dumb Forgetfulness a prey,
　This pleasing anxious being e'er resign'd,
Left the warm precincts of the cheerful day,
　Nor cast one longing ling'ring look behind?

On some fond breast the parting soul relies,
　Some pious drops the closing eye requires;
Ev'n from the tomb the voice of Nature cries,
　Ev'n in our Ashes live their wonted Fires.

For thee, who mindful of th' unhonour'd Dead,
　Dost in these lines their artless tale relate;
If chance, by lonely contemplation led,
　Some kindred Spirit shall inquire thy fate.

Haply some hoary-headed Swain may say,
  'Oft have we seen him at the peep of dawn
'Brushing with hasty steps the dews away
  'To meet the sun upon the upland lawn.

'There at the foot of yonder nodding beech
  'That wreathes its old fantastic roots so high,
'His listless length at noontide would he stretch,
  'And pore upon the brook that babbles by.

'Hard by yon wood, now smiling as in scorn,
  'Mutt'ring his wayward fancies he would rove,
'Now drooping, woeful wan, like one forlorn,
  'Or craz'd with care, or cross'd in hopeless love.

'One morn I missed him on the custom'd hill,
  'Along the heath and near his fav'rite tree;
'Another came; nor yet beside the rill,
  'Nor up the lawn, nor at the wood was he;

'The next with dirges due in sad array
  'Slow thro the church-way path we saw him borne.
'Approach and read (for thou can'st read) the lay,
  'Grav'd on the stone beneath yon aged thorn.'

THE EPITAPH

Here rests his head upon the lap of Earth
  A Youth to Fortune and to Fame unknown.
Fair Science frown'd not on his humble birth,
  And Melancholy mark'd him for her own.

Large was his bounty, and his soul sincere,
  Heav'n did a recompense as largely send:
He gave to Mis'ry all he had, a tear,
  He gain'd from Heav'n ('twas all he wish'd) a friend.

No farther seek his merits to disclose,
  Or draw his frailties from their dread abode,—
(There they alike in trembling hope repose),
  The bosom of his Father and his God.

Cuddle Doon

ALEXANDER ANDERSON
(Born April 30, 1845; died July 11, 1909)

The bairnies cuddle doon at nicht
  Wi' muckle fash an' din.
"Oh, try and sleep, ye waukrife rogues;
  Your faither's comin' in."
They never heed a word I speak.
  I try to gie a froon;
But aye I hap them up, an' cry,
  "Oh, bairnies, cuddle doon!"

Wee Jaimie wi' the curly heid—
  He aye sleeps next the wa'—
Bangs up an' cries, "I want a piece"—
  The rascal starts them a'.
I rin an' fetch them pieces, drinks—
  They stop awee the soun'—
Then draw the blankets up, an' cry,
  "Noo, weanies, cuddle doon!"

But ere five minutes gang, wee Rab
  Cries oot, frae 'neath the claes,
"Mither, mak' Tam gie ower at ance:
  He's kittlin' wi' his taes."
The mischief's in that Tam for tricks;
  He'd bother half the toon.
But aye I hap them up, an' cry,
  "Oh, bairnies, cuddle doon!"

At length they hear their father's fit;
  An', as he steeks the door,
They turn their faces to the wa',
  While Tam pretends to snore.

"Hae a' the weans been gude?" he asks,
  As he pits aff his shoon.
"The bairnies, John, are in their beds,
  An' lang since cuddled doon."

An' just afore we bed oorsels,
  We look at oor wee lambs.
Tam has his airm roun' wee Rab's neck,
  An' Rab his airm roun' Tam's.
I lift wee Jaimie up the bed,
  An, as I straik each croon,
I whisper, till my heart fills up,
  "Oh, bairnies, cuddle doon!"

The bairnies cuddle doon at nicht
  Wi' mirth that's dear to me;
But soon the big warl's cark an' care
  Will quaten doon their glee.
Yet, come what will to ilka ane,
  May He who rules aboon
Aye whisper, through their pows be bald,
  "Oh, bairnies, cuddle doon!"

Bettmann

Thanatopsis

WILLIAM CULLEN BRYANT
(Born November 3, 1794; died June 12, 1878)

To him who, in the love of Nature, holds
Communion with her visible forms, she speaks
A various language: for his gayer hours
She has a voice of gladness, and a smile
And eloquence of beauty; and she glides
Into his darker musings, with a mild
And healing sympathy, that steals away
Their sharpness, ere he is aware. When thoughts
Of the last bitter hour come like a blight
Over thy spirit, and sad images

Of the stern agony, and shroud, and pall,
And breathless darkness, and the narrow house,
Make thee to shudder, and grow sick at heart,—
Go forth under the open sky, and list
To Nature's teachings, while from all around—
Earth and her waters, and the depths of air—
Comes a still voice:—Yet a few days, and thee
The all-beholding sun shall see no more
In all his course; nor yet in the cold ground,
Where thy pale form was laid, with many tears,
Nor in the embrace of ocean, shall exist
Thy image. Earth, that nourished thee, shall claim
Thy growth, to be resolved to earth again;
And, lost each human trace, surrendering up
Thine individual being, shalt thou go
To mix forever with the elements;
To be a brother to the insensible rock,
And to the sluggish clod, which the rude swain
Turns with his share, and treads upon. The oak
Shall send his roots abroad, and pierce thy mold.
Yet not to thine eternal resting place
Shalt thou retire alone—nor couldst thou wish
Couch more magnificent. Thou shalt lie down
With patriarchs of the infant world—with kings,
The powerful of the earth—the wise, the good,
Fair forms, and hoary seers of ages past,
All in one mighty sepulcher. The hills,
Rock-ribbed, and ancient as the sun; the vales
Stretching in pensive quietness between;
The venerable woods; rivers that move
In majesty, and the complaining brooks,
That make the meadows green, and, poured round all
Old ocean's gray and melancholy waste—
Are but the solemn decorations all
Of the great tomb of man! The golden sun,
The planets, all the infinite host of heaven,
Are shining on the sad abodes of death,
Through the still lapse of ages. All that tread
The globe are but a handful to the tribes
That slumber in its bosom. Take the wings
Of morning, pierce the Barcan wilderness,
Or lose thyself in the continuous woods
Where rolls the Oregon and hears no sound
Save his own dashings—yet the dead are there;
And millions in those solitudes, since first

The flight of years began, have laid them down
In their last sleep—the dead reign there alone!
So shalt thou rest, and what if thou withdraw
In silence from the living; and no friend
Take note of thy departure? All that breathe
Will share thy destiny. The gay will laugh
When thou art gone, the solemn brood of care
Plod on, and each one as before shall chase
His favorite phantom; yet all these shall leave
Their mirth and their employments, and shall come
And make their bed with thee. As the long train
Of ages glides away, the sons of men—
The youth in life's green spring, and he who goes
In the full strength of years, matron and maid,
And the sweet babe, and the gray-headed man—
Shall one by one be gathered to thy side,
By those, who in their turn shall follow them.

So live that when thy summons comes to join
The innumerable caravan that moves
To that mysterious realm, where each shall take
His chamber in the silent halls of death,
Thou go not, like the quarry-slave at night,
Scourged to his dungeon, but, sustained and soothed
By an unfaltering trust, approach thy grave
Like one who wraps the drapery of his couch
About him, and lies down to pleasant dreams.

By special permission of D. Appleton & Company.

Bettmann

The Children's Hour

HENRY WADSWORTH LONGFELLOW
(Born February 27, 1807; died March 24, 1882)

Between the dark and the daylight,
    When the light is beginning to lower,
Comes a pause in the day's occupations
    That is known as the Children's Hour.

I hear in the chamber above me
    The patter of little feet,
The sound of a door that is opened,
    And voices soft and sweet.

From my study I see in the lamplight,
    Descending the broad hall stair,
Grave Alice and laughing Allegra,
    And Edith with golden hair.

A whisper, and then a silence;
    Yet I know by their merry eyes,
They are plotting and planning together
    To take me by surprise.

A sudden rush from the stairway,
    A sudden raid from the hall!
By three doors left unguarded
    They enter my castle wall!

They climb up into my turret,
    O'er the arms and back of my chair;
If I try to escape, they surround me;
    They seem to be everywhere.

They almost devour me with kisses,
    Their arms about me entwine,

Till I think of the Bishop of Bingen
In his Mouse-Tower on the Rhine.

Do you think, O blue-eyed banditti,
  Because you have scaled the wall,
Such an old mustache as I am
  Is not a match for you all?

I have you fast in my fortress,
  And will not let you depart,
But put you down into the dungeon
  In the round-tower of my heart.

And there will I keep you forever,
  Yes, forever and a day,
Till the wall shall crumble to ruin,
  And moulder in dust away.

Bettmann

Summum Bonum

ROBERT BROWNING
(Born May 7, 1812; died December 12, 1889)

All the breath and the bloom of the
    year in the bag of one bee:
All the wonder and wealth of the mine in
    the heart of one gem:
In the core of one pearl all the shade and the
    shine of the sea:
Breath and bloom, shade and shine,—wonder,
    wealth, and—how far above them—
      Truth, that's brighter than gem,
      Trust, that's purer than pearl,—
Brightest truth, purest trust in the universe—
    all were for me
      In the kiss of one girl.

By special permission of the Houghton-Mifflin Co.

Bettmann

Horatius

Thomas Babington Macaulay
(Born October 25, 1800; died December 28, 1859)

Lars Porsena of Clusium
   By the nine gods he swore
That the great house of Tarquin
   Should suffer wrong no more.
By the nine gods he swore it,
   And named a trysting day,
And bade his messengers ride forth,
East and west and south and north,
   To summon his array.

East and west and south and north
   The messengers ride fast,
And tower and town and cottage
   Have heard the trumpet's blast.
The horsemen and the footmen
   Are pouring in amain
From many a stately market-place,
   From many a fruitful plain;

* * * *

And now hath every city
   Sent up her tale of men;
The foot are fourscore thousand
   The horse are thousands ten.
Before the gates of Sutrium
   Is met the great array,
A proud man was Lars Porsena
   Upon the trysting day.

* * * *

But by the yellow Tiber
  Was tumult and affright:
From all the spacious champaign
  To Rome men took their flight.
A mile around the city,
  The throng stopped up the ways;
A fearful sight it was to see
  Through two long nights and days.

*   *   *   *

Now, from the rock Tarpeian,
  Could the wan burghers spy
The line of blazing villages
  Red in the midnight sky.
The Fathers of the City,
  They sat all night and day
For every hour some horseman came
  With tidings of dismay.

*   *   *   *

They held a council standing
  Before the river-gate;
Short time was there, ye well may guess,
  For musing or debate.
Outspake the Consul roundly:
  "The bridge must straight go down;
For since Janiculum is lost
  Naught else can save the town."

Just then a scout came flying,
  All wild with haste and fear:
"To arms! to arms! Sir Consul;
  Lars Porsena is here."
On the low hills to westward
  The Consul fixed his eye,
And saw the swarthy storm of dust
  Rise fast along the sky.

And nearer, fast and nearer,
  Doth the red whirlwind come;
And louder still and still more loud,
From underneath that rolling cloud,
Is heard the trumpet's war-note proud,

The trampling and the hum.
And plainly and more plainly
  Now through the gloom appears,
Far to left and far to right,
In broken gleams of dark-blue light,
The long array of helmets bright,
  The long array of spears.

*   *   *   *

But the Consul's brow was sad,
  And the Consul's speech was low,
And darkly looked he at the wall,
  And darkly at the foe:
"Their van will be upon us
  Before the bridge goes down;
And if they once may win the bridge
  What hope to save the town?"

Then outspake brave Horatius.
  The captain of the gate:
"To every man upon this earth
  Death cometh soon or late.
And how can man die better
  Than facing fearful odds
For the ashes of his fathers
  And the temples of his gods?

"Hew down the bridge, Sir Consul,
  With all the speed ye may;
I, with two more to help me,
  Will hold the foe in play,—
In yon strait path a thousand
  May well be stopped by three.
Now who will stand on either hand,
  And keep the bridge with me?"

Then outspake Spurius Lartius,—
  A Ramnian proud was he:
"Lo, I will stand at thy right hand,
  And keep the bridge with thee."
And outspake strong Herminius,—
  Of Titian blood was he:
"I will abide on thy left side,
  And keep the bridge with thee."

"Horatius," quoth the Consul,
  "As thou sayest, so let it be."
And straight against that great array,
  Forth went the dauntless Three.
Now, while the Three were tightening
  Their harness on their backs,
The Consul was the foremost man
  To take in hand an axe;
And Fathers mixed with Commons
  Seized hatchet, bar, and crow,
And smote upon the planks above,
  And loosed the props below.

*   *   *   *

Meanwhile the Tuscan army,
  Right glorious to behold,
Came flashing back the noonday light,
Rank behind rank, like surges bright
  Of a broad sea of gold.
Four hundred trumpets sounded
  A peal of warlike glee,
As that great host, with measured tread,
And spears advanced, and ensigns spread,
Rolled slowly toward the bridge's head,
  Where stood the dauntless Three.

The Three stood calm and silent,
  And looked upon the foes,
And a great shout of laughter
  From all the vanguard rose;
And forth three chiefs came spurring
  Before the mighty mass;
To earth they sprang, their swords they drew,
And lifted high their shields, and flew
  To win the narrow pass.

Aunus, from green Tifernum,
  Lord of the hill of vines;
And Seius, whose eight hundred slaves
  Sicken in Ilva's mines;
And Picus, long to Clusium
  Vassal in peace and war,
Who led to fight his Umbrian powers
From that grey crag where, girt with towers,

The fortress of Nequinum towers
   O'er the pale waves of Nar.

Stout Lartius hurled down Aunus
   Into the stream beneath;
Herminius struck at Seius,
   And clove him to the teeth;
At Picus brave Horatius
   Darted one fiery thrust,
And the proud Umbrian's gilded arms
   Clashed in the bloody dust.

*   *   *   *

But now no sound of laughter
   Was heard amongst the foes.
A wild and wrathful clamor
   From all the vanguard rose.
Six spears' lengths from the entrance
   Halted that mighty mass,
And for a space no man came forth
   To win the narrow pass.

But, hark! the cry is Astur:
   And lo! the ranks divide;
And the great lord of Luna
   Comes with his stately stride.
Upon his ample shoulders
   Clangs loud the fourfold shield,
And in his hand he shakes the brand
   Which none but he can wield.

He smiled on those bold Romans,
   A smile serene and high;
He eyed the flinching Tuscans,
   And scorn was in his eye.
Quoth he, "The she-wolf's litter
   Stand savagely at bay;
But will ye dare to follow,
   If Astur clears the way?"

Then, whirling up his broadsword
   With both hands to the height,
He rushed against Horatius,
   And smote with all his might,

With shield and blade Horatius
  Right deftly turned the blow,
The blow, though turned, came yet too nigh;
It missed his helm, but gashed his thigh.
The Tuscans raised a joyful cry
  To see the red blood flow.

He reeled, and on Herminius
  He leaned one breathing-space,
Then, like a wild-cat mad with wounds,
  Sprang right at Astur's face.
Through teeth and skull and helmet
  So fierce a thrust he sped,
The good sword stood a handbreadth out
  Behind the Tuscan's head.

And the great lord of Luna
  Fell at that deadly stroke,
As falls on Mount Avernus
  A thunder-smitten oak.
Far o'er the crashing forest
  The giant arms lie spread;
And the pale augurs, muttering low,
  Gaze on the blasted head.

On Astur's throat Horatius
  Right firmly pressed his heel,
And thrice and four times tugged amain,
Ere he wrenched out the steel.
"And see," he cried, "the welcome,
  Fair guests, that waits you here!
What noble Lucumo comes next
  To taste our Roman cheer?"

*   *   *   *

But meanwhile axe and lever
  Have manfully been plied,
And now the bridge hangs tottering
  Above the boiling tide.
"Come back, come back, Horatius!"
  Loud cried the Fathers all;
"Back, Lartius! back, Herminius!
  Back, ere the ruin fall!"

Back darted Spurius Lartius;
   Herminius darted back;
And, as they passed, beneath their feet
   They felt the timbers crack;
But when they turned their faces,
   And on the further shore
Saw brave Horatius stand alone,
   They would have crossed once more.

But, with a crash like thunder
   Fell every loosened beam,
And, like a dam, the mighty wreck
   Lay right athwart the stream;
And a long shout of triumph
   Rose from the walls of Rome,
As to the highest turret-tops
   Was splashed the yellow foam.

      *   *   *   *

Alone stood brave Horatius,
   But constant still in mind,—
Thrice thirty thousand foes before,
   And the broad flood behind,
"Down with him!" cried false Sextus,
   With a smile on his pale face;
"Now yield thee," cried Lars Porsena,
   "Now yield thee to our grace!"

Round turned he, as not deigning
   Those craven ranks to see;
Naught spake he to Lars Porsena,
   To Sextus naught spake he;
But he saw on Palatinus
   The white porch of his home;
And he spake to the noble river
   That rolls by the towers of Rome:

"O Tiber! Father Tiber!
   To whom the Romans pray
A Roman's life, a Roman's arms,
   Take thou in charge this day!"
So he spake, and, speaking, sheathed
   The good sword by his side,

107

And, with his harness on his back,
　　Plunged headlong in the tide.

No sound of joy or sorrow
　　Was heard from either bank,
But friends and foes in dumb surprise,
With parted lips and straining eyes,
　　Stood gazing where he sank;
And when above the surges
　　They saw his crest appear,
All Rome sent forth a rapturous cry,
And even the ranks of Tuscany
　　Could scarce forbear to cheer.

But fiercely ran the current,
　　Swollen high by months of rain,
And fast his blood was flowing;
　　And he was sore in pain,
And heavy with his armor,
　　And spent with changing blows;
And oft they thought him sinking,
　　But still again he rose.

　　　*　　*　　*　　*

And now he feels the bottom;—
　　Now on dry earth he stands;
Now round him throng the Fathers
　　To press his gory hands.
And, now, with shouts and clapping,
　　And noise of weeping loud,
He enters through the River Gate,
　　Borne by the joyous crowd.

Bettmann

Sea Fever

JOHN MASEFIELD

*(Born Ledbury, Herefordshire, England, June 1,
1878; died May 12, 1967)*

I must go down to the seas again, to the
   lonely sea and the sky,
And all I ask is a tall ship and a star to steer
   her by;
And the wheel's kick and the wind's song and
   the white sail's shaking,
And a grey mist on the sea's face, and a grey
   dawn breaking.

I must go down to the seas again, for the call
   of the running tide
Is a wild call and a clear call that may not be
   denied;
And all I ask is a windy day with the white
   clouds flying,
And the flung spray and the blown spume, and
   the sea-gulls crying.

I must go down to the seas again, to the
   vagrant gypsy life,
To the gull's way and the whale's way, where
   the wind's like a whetted knife;
And all I ask is a merry yarn from a laughing
   fellow-rover,
And quiet sleep and a sweet dream when the
   long trick's over.

Bettmann

The Eternal Goodness

JOHN GREENLEAF WHITTIER
*(Born December 17, 1807;
died September 7, 1892)*

O friends! with whom my feet have trod
  The quiet aisles of prayer,
Glad witness to your zeal for God
  And love of man I bear.

I trace your lines of argument;
  Your logic linked and strong
I weigh as one who dreads dissent,
  And fears a doubt as wrong.

But still my human hands are weak
  To hold your iron creeds:
Against the words ye bid me speak
  My heart within me pleads.

Who fathoms the Eternal Thought?
  Who talks of scheme and plan?
The Lord is God! He needeth not
  The poor device of man.

I walk with bare, hushed feet the ground
  Ye tread with boldness shod;
I dare not fix with mete and bound
  The love and power of God.

Ye praise His justice; even such
  His pitying love I deem:
Ye seek a king; I fain would touch
  The robe that hath no seam.

Ye see the curse which overbroods
  A world of pain and loss;

I hear our Lord's beatitudes
　　And prayer upon the cross.

More than your schoolmen teach, within
　　Myself, alas! I know:
Too dark ye cannot paint the sin,
　　Too small the merit show.

I bow my forehead to the dust,
　　I veil mine eyes for shame,
And urge, in trembling self-distrust,
　　A prayer without a claim.

I see the wrong that round me lies,
　　I feel the guilt within;
I hear, with groan and travail-cries,
　　The world confess its sin.

Yet, in the maddening maze of things,
　　And tossed by storm and flood,
To one fixed trust my spirit clings;
　　I know that God is good!

Not mine to look where cherubim
　　And seraphs may not see,
But nothing can be good in Him
　　Which evil is in me.

The wrong that pains my soul below
　　I dare not throne above,
I know not of His hate,—I know
　　His goodness and His love.

I dimly guess from blessings known
　　Of greater out of sight,
And, with the chastened Psalmist, own
　　His judgments too are right.

I long for household voices gone,
　　For vanished smiles I long,
But God hath led my dear ones on,
　　And He can do no wrong.

I know not what the future hath
　　Of marvel or surprise,

111

Assured alone that life and death
  His mercy underlies.

And if my heart and flesh are weak
  To bear an untried pain,
The bruised reed He will not break,
  But strengthen and sustain.

No offering of my own I have,
  Nor works my faith to prove;
I can but give the gifts He gave,
  And plead His love for love.

And so beside the Silent Sea
  I wait the muffled oar;
No harm from Him can come to me
  On ocean or on shore.

I know not where His islands lift
  Their fronded palms in air;
I only know I cannot drift
  Beyond His love and care.

O brothers! if my faith is vain,
  If hopes like these betray,
Pray for me that my feet may gain
  The sure and safer way.

And Thou, O Lord! by whom are seen
  Thy creatures as they be,
Forgive me if too close I lean
  My human heart to Thee!

Bettmann

If

RUDYARD KIPLING
(Born December 30, 1865; died January 17, 1936)

If you can keep your head when all about you
    Are losing theirs and blaming it on you;
If you can trust yourself when all men doubt you,
    But make allowance for their doubting too:
If you can wait and not be tired by waiting,
    Or being lied about, don't deal in lies,
Or being hated don't give way to hating,
    And yet don't look too good, nor talk too wise;

If you can dream—and not make dreams your master;
    If you can think—and not make thoughts your aim,
If you can meet with Triumph and Disaster
    And treat those two impostors just the same:
If you can bear to hear the truth you've spoken
    Twisted by knaves to make a trap for fools,
Or watch the things you gave your life to, broken,
    And stoop and build 'em up with worn-out tools;

If you can make one heap of all your winnings
    And risk it on one turn of pitch-and-toss,
And lose, and start again at your beginnings,
    And never breathe a word about your loss:
If you can force your heart and nerve and sinew
    To serve your turn long after they are gone,
And so hold on when there is nothing in you
    Except the Will which says to them: "Hold on!"

If you can talk with crowds and keep your virtue,
    Or walk with Kings—nor lose the common touch,
If neither foes nor loving friends can hurt you,
    If all men count with you, but none too much:
If you can fill the unforgiving minute
    With sixty seconds' worth of distance run,
Yours is the Earth and everything that's in it,
    And—which is more—you'll be a Man, my son!

Bettmann

The Day Is Done

HENRY WADSWORTH LONGFELLOW
(Born February 27, 1807; died March 24, 1882)

The day is done, and the darkness
  Falls from the wings of Night,
As a feather is wafted downward
  From an eagle in his flight.

I see the lights of the village
  Gleam through the rain and the mist,
And a feeling of sadness comes o'er me
  That my soul cannot resist:

A feeling of sadness and longing,
  That is not akin to pain,
And resembles sorrow only
  As the mist resembles the rain.

Come, read to me some poem,
  Some simple and heartfelt lay,
That shall soothe this restless feeling,
  And banish the thoughts of day.

Not from the grand old masters
  Not from the bards sublime,
Whose distant footsteps echo
  Through the corridors of Time.

For, like strains of martial music,
  Their mighty thoughts suggest
Life's endless toil and endeavor;
  And tonight I long for rest.

Read from some humbler poet,
  Whose songs gushed from his heart,
As showers from the clouds of summer,
  Or tears from the eyelids start;

Who, through long days of labor,
  And nights devoid of ease,
Still heard in his soul the music
  Of wonderful melodies.

Such songs have power to quiet
  The restless pulse of care,
And come like the benediction
  That follows after prayer.

Then read from the treasured volume
  The poem of thy choice,
And lend to the rhyme of the poet
  The beauty of thy voice.

And the night shall be filled with music
  And the cares, that infest the day,
Shall fold their tents, like the Arabs,
  And as silently steal away.

Invictus

WILLIAM ERNEST HENLEY
(Born August 23, 1849; died July 11, 1903)

Out of the night that covers me,
  Black as the Pit from pole to pole,
I thank whatever gods may be
  For my unconquerable soul.

In the fell clutch of circumstance
  I have not winced nor cried aloud.
Under the bludgeonings of chance
  My head is bloody, but unbowed.

Beyond this place of wrath and tears
  Looms but the horror of the shade,

115

And yet the menace of the years
   Finds, and shall find me, unafraid.

It matters not how strait the gate,
   How charged with punishments the scroll,
I am the master of my fate;
   I am the captain of my soul.

Bettmann

Abou Ben Adhem

JAMES HENRY LEIGH HUNT
(Born October 19, 1784; died August 28, 1859)

Abou Ben Adhem (may his tribe increase!)
Awoke one night from a deep dream of peace,
And saw, within the moonlight in his room,
   Making it rich, and like a lily in bloom,
An Angel writing in a book of gold:
Exceeding peace had made Ben Adhem bold,
And to the Presence in the room he said,
"What writest thou?" The Vision raised its head,
And with a look made of all sweet accord
Answered, "The names of those who love the Lord."
"And is mine one?" said Abou. "Nay, not so,"
Replied the Angel. Abou spoke more low,
But cheerly still; and said, "I pray thee, then,
Write me as one that loves his fellow-men."

The Angel wrote, and vanished. The next night
It came again with a great wakening light,
And showed the names whom love of God had blessed,
And, lo! Ben Adhem's name led all the rest!

Bettmann

Nobility

ALICE CARY

(Born April 26, 1820; died February 12, 1871)

True worth is in *being*, not *seeming*,—
  In doing, each day that goes by,
Some little good—not in dreaming
  Of great things to do by and by.
For whatever men say in their blindness,
  And spite of the fancies of youth,
There's nothing so kingly as kindness,
  And nothing so royal as truth.

We get back our mete as we measure—
  We cannot do wrong and feel right,
Nor can we give pain and gain pleasure,
  For justice avenges each slight.
The air for the wing of the sparrow,
  The bush for the robin and wren,
But always the path that is narrow
  And straight, for the children of men.

'Tis not in the pages of story
  The heart of its ills to beguile,
Though he who makes courtship to glory
  Gives all that he hath for her smile.
For when from her heights he has won her,
  Alas! it is only to prove
That nothing's so sacred as honor,
  And nothing so loyal as love!

We cannot make bargains for blisses,
  Nor catch them like fishes in nets;
And sometimes the thing our life misses
  Helps more than the thing which it gets.
For good lieth not in pursuing,

Nor gaining of great nor of small,
But just in the doing, and doing
    As we would be done by, is all.

Through envy, through malice, through hating,
    Against the world, early and late,
No jot of our courage abating—
    Our part is to work and to wait.
And slight is the sting of his trouble
    Whose winnings are less than his worth;
For he who is honest is noble,
    Whatever his fortunes or birth.

Each in His Own Tongue

WILLIAM HERBERT CARRUTH
(Born April 5, 1859; died December 15, 1924)

A fire-mist and a planet,
    A crystal and a cell,
A jelly-fish and a saurian,
    And caves where the cave-men dwell;
Then a sense of law and beauty
    And a face turned from the clod—
Some call it Evolution,
    And others call it God.

A haze on the far horizon,
    The infinite, tender sky,
The ripe rich tint of the cornfields,
    And the wild geese sailing high—
And all over upland and lowland
    The charm of the golden-rod—
Some of us call it Autumn
    And others call it God.

118

Like tides on a crescent sea-beach,
  When the moon is new and thin,
Into our hearts high yearnings
  Come welling and surging in—
Come from the mystic ocean,
  Whose rim no foot has trod,—
Some of us call it Longing,
  And others call it God.

A picket frozen on duty,
  A mother starved for her brood,
Socrates drinking the hemlock,
  And Jesus on the rood;
And millions who, humble and nameless,
  The straight, hard pathway plod,—
Some call it Consecration,
  And others call it God.

From *Each in His Own Tongue and Other Poems*. G. P. Putnam's Sons, New York.

Bettmann

Childe Harold's Farewell to England

GEORGE GORDON BYRON
(Sixth Lord)
(Born January 22, 1788; died April 19, 1824)

Adieu, adieu! my native shore
  Fades o'er the waters blue;
The night-winds sigh, the breakers roar,
  And shrieks the wild sea-mew.
Yon sun that sets upon the sea,
  We follow in his flight;
Farewell awhile to him and thee,
  My native land—Good-night.

A few short hours and he will rise
  To give the morrow birth;
And I shall hail the main and skies,

119

But not my mother earth.
Deserted is my own good hall,
  Its hearth is desolate;
Wild weeds are gathering on the wall;
  My dog howls at the gate.

Come hither, hither, my little page!
  Why does thou weep and wail?
Or dost thou dread the billow's rage,
  Or tremble at the gale?
But dash the tear-drop from thine eye;
  Our ship is swift and strong;
Our fleetest falcon scarce can fly
  More merrily along.

"Let winds be shrill, let waves roll high,
  I fear not wave nor wind:
Yet marvel not, Sir Childe, that I
  Am sorrowful in mind;
For I have from my father gone,
  A mother whom I love,
And have no friends, save these alone,
  But thee—and One above.

"My father blessed me fervently,
  Yet did not much complain;
But sorely will my mother sigh
  Till I come back again."—
Enough, enough, my little lad!
  Such tears become thine eye;
If I thy guileless bosom had,
  Mine own would not be dry.

*   *   *   *

Bettmann

God Save the Flag

OLIVER WENDELL HOLMES

(Born August 29, 1809; died October 7, 1894)

Washed in the blood of the brave and the blooming,
   Snatched from the altars of insolent foes,
Burning with star-fires, but never consuming,
   Flash its broad ribbons of lily and rose.

Vainly the prophets of Baal would rend it,
   Vainly his worshippers pray for its fall;
Thousands have died for it, millions defend it,
   Emblem of justice and mercy to all:

Justice that reddens the sky with her terrors,
   Mercy that comes with her white-handed train,
Soothing all passions, redeeming all errors,
   Sheathing the sabre and breaking the chain.

Borne on the deluge of old usurpations,
   Drifted our Ark o'er the desolate seas,
Bearing the rainbow of hope to the nations,
   Torn from the storm-cloud and flung to the breeze!

God bless the Flag and its loyal defenders,
   While its broad folds o'er the battle-field wave,
Till the dim star-wreath rekindle its splendors,
   Washed from its stains in the blood of the brave!

Bettmann

The Minuet

MARY MAPES DODGE
(Born January 26, 1838; died August 21, 1905)

Grandma told me all about it,
Told me so I couldn't doubt it,
How she danced, my grandma danced; long ago—
How she held her pretty head,
How her dainty skirt she spread,
How she slowly leaned and rose—long ago.

Grandma's hair was bright and sunny,
Dimpled cheeks, too, oh, how funny!
Really quite a pretty girl—long ago.
Bless her! why, she wears a cap,
Grandma does, and takes a nap
Every single day: and yet
Grandma danced the minuet—long ago.

"Modern ways are quite alarming,"
Grandma says, "but boys were charming"
(Girls and boys she means, of course) "long ago."
Brave but modest, grandly shy;
She would like to have us try
Just to feel like those who met
In the graceful minuet—long ago.

From *Along the Way*. Copyright 1879. Published by Charles Scribner's Sons.

Bettmann

That Time of Year

WILLIAM SHAKESPEARE
(Born April 23[?], 1564; died April 23, 1616)

That time of year thou may'st in me behold
  When yellow leaves, or none, or few, do hang
Upon those boughs which shake against the cold,
  Bare ruin'd choirs, where late the sweet birds sang:

In me thou see'st the twilight of such day
  As after sunset fadeth in the west,
Which by and by black night doth take away,
  Death's second self, that seals up all in rest:

In me thou see'st the glowing of such fire
  That on the ashes of his youth doth lie,
As the death-bed whereon it must expire,
  Consum'd with that which it was nourish'd by:

—This thou perceiv'st, which makes thy love more
    strong,
To love that well which thou must leave ere long.

Bettmann

The Raven

EDGAR ALLEN POE

(Born January 19, 1809; died October 7, 1849)

Once upon a midnight dreary, while I pondered, weak and weary,
Over many a quaint and curious volume of forgotten lore,
While I nodded, nearly napping, suddenly there came a tapping,
As of someone gently rapping, rapping at my chamber door.
" 'Tis some visitor," I muttered, "tapping at my chamber door;
      Only this, and nothing more."

Ah, distinctly I remember, it was in the bleak December,
And each separate dying ember wrought its ghost upon the floor.
Eagerly I wished the morrow; vainly I had sought to borrow
From my books surcease of sorrow, sorrow for the lost Lenore,
For the rare and radiant maiden whom the angels name Lenore,
      Nameless here forevermore.

And the silken sad uncertain rustling of each purple curtain
Thrilled me—filled me with fantastic terrors never felt before;
So that now, to still the beating of my heart, I stood repeating,
" 'Tis some visitor entreating entrance at my chamber door,
Some late visitor entreating entrance at my chamber door;
      This it is, and nothing more."

Presently my soul grew stronger; hesitating then no longer,
"Sir," said I, "or madam, truly your forgiveness I implore;
But the fact is, I was napping, and so gently you came rapping,
And so faintly you came tapping, tapping at my chamber door,
That I scarce was sure I heard you." Here I opened wide the door;—
      Darkness there, and nothing more.

Deep into the darkness peering, long I stood there, wondering,
    fearing,
Doubting, dreaming dreams no mortals ever dared to dream before;
But the silence was unbroken, and the stillness gave no token,

And the only word there spoken was the whispered word, "Lenore?"
This I whispered, and an echo murmured back the word, "Lenore!"
 Merely this, and nothing more.

Back into the chamber turning, all my soul within me burning,
Soon again I heard a tapping, something louder than before,
"Surely," said I, "surely, that is something at my window lattice;
Let me see, then, what thereat is, and this mystery explore;
Let my heart be still a moment, and this mystery explore;
 'Tis the wind, and nothing more."

Open here I flung the shutter, when, with many a flirt and flutter,
In there stepped a stately raven, of the saintly days of yore.
Not the least obeisance made he; not a minute stopped or stayed he;
But with mien of lord or lady, perched above my chamber door;
Perched upon a bust of Pallas, just above my chamber door,
 Perched, and sat, and nothing more.

Then this ebony bird beguiling my sad fancy into smiling,
By the grave and stern decorum of the countenance it wore,
"Though thy crest be shorn and shaven, thou," I said, "art sure no
 craven,
Ghastly, grim, and ancient raven, wandering from the nightly shore,
Tell me what thy lordly name is on the Night's Plutonian shore."
 Quoth the raven, "Nevermore."

Much I marvelled this ungainly fowl to hear discourse so plainly,
Though its answer little meaning, little relevancy bore;
For we cannot help agreeing that no living human being
Ever yet was blessed with seeing bird above his chamber door,
Bird or beast upon the sculptured bust above his chamber door,
 With such name as "Nevermore."

But the raven, sitting lonely on that placid bust, spoke only
That one word, as if his soul in that one word he did outpour.
Nothing further then he uttered; not a feather then he fluttered;
Till I scarcely more than muttered, "Other friends have flown be-
 fore;
On the morrow *he* will leave me, as my hopes have flown before."
 Then the bird said, "Nevermore."

Startled at the stillness broken by reply so aptly spoken,
"Doubtless," said I, "what it utters is its only stock and store,
Caught from some unhappy master, whom unmerciful disaster
Followed fast and followed faster, till his songs one burden bore,—

125

Till the dirges of his hope that melancholy burden bore
       Of "Never—nevermore."

But the raven still beguiling all my fancy into smiling,
Straight I wheeled a cushioned seat in front of bird and bust and
    door;
Then, upon the velvet sinking, I betook myself to linking
Fancy unto fancy, thinking what this ominous bird of yore,
What this grim, ungainly, ghastly, gaunt, and ominous bird of yore
       Meant in croaking, "Nevermore."

Thus I sat engaged in guessing, but no syllable expressing
To the fowl, whose fiery eyes now burned into my bosom's core;
This and more I sat divining, with my head at ease reclining
On the cushion's velvet lining that the lamplight gloated o'er,
But whose velvet violet lining with the lamplight gloating o'er
       She shall press, ah, nevermore!

Then, methought, the air grew denser, perfumed from an unseen
    censer
Swung by seraphim whose footfalls tinkled on the tufted floor.
"Wretch," I cried, "thy God hath lent thee—by these angels he hath
    sent thee
Respite—respite and nepenthe from thy memories of Lenore!
Quaff, O quaff this kind nepenthe, and forget this lost Lenore!"
       Quoth the raven, "Nevermore!"

"Prophet!" said I, "thing of evil!—prophet still, if bird or devil!
Whether tempter sent, or whether tempest tossed thee here ashore,
Desolate, yet all undaunted, on this desert land enchanted—
On this home by horror haunted—tell me truly, I implore:
Is there—*is* there balm in Gilead!—tell me—tell me I implore!"
       Quoth the raven, "Nevermore."

"Prophet!" said I, "thing of evil—prophet still, if bird or devil!
By that heaven that bends above us—by that God we both adore—
Tell this soul with sorrow laden, if, within the distant Aidenn,
It shall clasp a sainted maiden, whom the angels name Lenore—
Clasp a rare and radiant maiden, whom the angels name Lenore?
       Quoth the raven, "Nevermore."

"Be that word our sign of parting, bird or fiend!" I shrieked,
    upstarting—
"Get thee back into the tempest and the Night's Plutonian shore!
Leave no black plume as a token of that lie thy soul hath spoken!

Leave my loneliness unbroken!—quit the bust above my door!
Take thy beak from out my heart, and take thy form from off my
    door!"
        Quoth the raven, "Nevermore."

And the raven, never flitting, still is sitting, still is sitting
On the pallid bust of Pallas just above my chamber door;
And his eyes have all the seeming of a demon's that is dreaming;
And the lamplight o'er him streaming throws the shadow on the
    floor;
And my soul from out that shadow that lies floating on the floor
        Shall be lifted—nevermore!

Bettmann

Love of Country

From "The Lay of the Last Minstrel"

SIR WALTER SCOTT
(Born August 15, 1771; died September 21, 1832)

Breathes there the man with soul so dead
Who never to himself hath said:
    "This is my own, my native land"?
Whose heart hath ne'er within him burned
As home his footsteps he hath turned,
    From wandering on a foreign strand?
If such there breathe, go mark him well;
For him no minstrel raptures swell;
High though his titles, proud his name,
Boundless his wealth as wish can claim;
Despite those titles, power and pelf,
The wretch concentred all in self,
Living, shall forfeit fair renown,
And, doubly dying, shall go down
To the vile dust from whence he sprung,
Unwept, unhonored, and unsung.

The Highwayman

ALFRED NOYES
(Born September 16, 1880; died June 29, 1958)

PART ONE

The wind was a torrent of darkness among the gusty trees,
The moon was a ghostly galleon tossed upon cloudy seas,
The road was a ribbon of moonlight over the purple moor,
    And the highwayman came riding,
    Riding, riding,
The highwayman came riding, up to the old inn-door.

He'd a French cocked-hat on his forehead, a bunch of lace at his
    chin,
A coat of the claret velvet, and breeches of brown doe-skin;
They fitted with never a wrinkle: his boots were up to the thigh!
    And he rode with a jeweled twinkle,
    His pistol butts a-twinkle,
His rapier hilt a-twinkle, under the jeweled sky.

Over the cobbles he clattered and clashed in the dark inn-yard,
And he tapped with his whip on the shutters, but all was locked and
    barred;
He whistled a tune to the window, and who should be waiting there
    But the landlord's black-eyed daughter,
    Bess, the landlord's daughter,
Plaiting a dark red love-knot into her long black hair.

And dark in the dark old inn-yard a stable-wicket creaked
Where Tim the ostler listened, his face was white and peaked;
His eyes were hollows of madness, his hair like mouldy hay,
    But he loved the landlord's daughter,
    The landlord's red-lipped daughter,
Dumb as a dog he listened, and he heard the robber say:

"One kiss, my bonny sweetheart, I'm after a prize tonight,
But I shall be back with the yellow gold before the morning light;

Yet, if they press me sharply, and harry me through the day,
      Then look for me by moonlight,
      Watch for me by moonlight,
I'll come to thee by moonlight, though hell should bar the way."

He rose upright in the stirrups; he scarce could reach her hand,
But she loosened her hair i' the casement! His face burnt like a
      brand
As the black cascade of perfume came tumbling over his breast;
      And he kissed its waves in the moonlight,
      (Oh, sweet black waves in the moonlight!)
Then he tugged at his rein in the moonlight, and galloped away to
      the West.

PART TWO

He did not come in the dawning: he did not come at noon;
And out o' the tawny sunset, before the rise o' the moon,
When the road was a gypsy's ribbon, looping the purple moor,
      A red-coat troop came marching,
      Marching, marching,
King George's men came marching, up to the old inn-door.

They said no word to the landlord, they drank his ale instead,
But they gagged his daughter and bound her to the foot of her
      narrow bed;
Two of them knelt at her casement, with muskets at their side!
      There was death at every window;
      And hell at one dark window;
For Bess could see, through her casement, the road that *he* would
      ride.

They had tied her up to attention, with many a sniggering jest;
They had bound a musket beside her, with the barrel beneath her
      breast!
"Now keep good watch!" and they kissed her.   •
She heard the dead man say—
      Look for me by moonlight;
      Watch for me by moonlight;
I'll come to thee by moonlight, though hell should bar the way!

She twisted her hands behind her; but all the knots held good!
She writhed her hands till her fingers were wet with sweat or blood!
They stretched and strained in the darkness, and the hours crawled
      by like years,
      Till, now, on the stroke of midnight,

129

Cold, on the stroke of midnight,
The tip of one finger touched it! The trigger at least was hers!

The tip of one finger touched it; she strove no more for the rest!
Up, she stood up to attention, with the barrel beneath her breast,
She would not risk their hearing! she would not strive again;
For the road lay bare in the moonlight,
Blank and bare in the moonlight;
And the blood of her veins in the moonlight throbbed to her love's
refrain.

Tlot-tlot, tlot-tlot! Had they heard it? The horse-hoofs ringing clear;
Tlot-tlot, tlot-tlot, in the distance? Were they deaf that they did not
hear?
Down the ribbon of moonlight, over the brow of the hill,
The highwayman came riding,
Riding, riding!
The red-coats looked to their priming! She stood up, straight and
still!
Tlot-tlot, in the frosty silence! *Tlot-tlot,* in the echoing night!
Nearer he came and nearer! Her face was like a light!
Her eyes grew wide for a moment! she drew one last deep breath,
Then her finger moved in the moonlight,
Her musket shattered the moonlight,
Shattered her breast in the moonlight and warned him—with her
death.

He turned; he spurred to the West; he did not know she stood
Bowed, with her head o'er the musket, drenched with her own red
blood!
Not till the dawn he heard it; his face grew grey to hear
How Bess, the landlord's daughter,
The landlord's black-eyed daughter,
Had watched for her love in the moonlight, and died in the darkness
there.

Back he spurred like a madman, shrieking a curse to the sky,
With the white road smoking behind him and his rapier brandished
high!
Blood-red were his spurs i' the golden noon; wine-red was his velvet
coat,
When they shot him down on the highway,
Down like a dog on the highway,
And he lay in his blood on the highway, with the bunch of lace at
his throat.

And still of a winter's night, they say, when the wind is in the trees,
When the moon is a ghostly galleon tossed upon cloudy seas,
When the road is a ribbon of moonlight over the purple moor,
A highwayman comes riding,
Riding, riding,
A highwayman comes riding, up to the old inn-door.

Over the cobbles he clatters and clangs in the dark inn-yard;
He taps with his whip on the shutters, but all is locked and barred;
He whistles a tune to the window, and who should be waiting there
But the landlord's black-eyed daughter,
Bess, the landlord's daughter,
Plaiting a dark red love-knot into her long black hair.

Bettmann

A Psalm of Life

HENRY WADSWORTH LONGFELLOW
(Born February 27, 1807, died March 24, 1882)

Tell me not, in mournful numbers,
Life is but an empty dream!—
For the soul is dead that slumbers,
And things are not what they seem.

Life is real! Life is earnest!
And the grave is not its goal;
Dust thou art, to dust returnest,
Was not spoken of the soul.

Not enjoyment, and not sorrow,
Is our destined end or way;
But to act, that each tomorrow
Find us farther than today.

Art is long, and Time is fleeting,
And our hearts, though stout and brave,

Still, like muffled drums, are beating
    Funeral marches to the grave.

In the world's broad field of battle,
    In the bivouac of life,
Be not like dumb, driven cattle!
    Be a hero in the strife!

Trust no Future, howe'er pleasant!
    Let the dead Past bury its dead!
Act,—act in the living Present!
    Heart within, and God o'erhead!

Lives of great men all remind us
    We can make our lives sublime,
And, departing, leave behind us
    Footprints on the sands of time.

Footprints, that perhaps another,
    Sailing o'er life's solemn main,
A forlorn and shipwrecked brother,
    Seeing, shall take heart again.

Let us then be up and doing,
    With a heart for any fate;
Still achieving, still pursuing,
    Learn to labor and to wait.

For A' That and A' That

ROBERT BURNS

(Born January 25, 1759; died July 21, 1796)

Is there, for honest poverty,
That hangs his head, and a' that?
The coward-slave, we pass him by;
We dare be poor for a' that!
For a' that, and a' that,
Our toils obscure, and a' that;
The rank is but the guinea stamp;
The man's the gowd for a' that.

What tho' on hamely fare we dine,
Wear hodden-gray, and a' that;
Gie fools their silks, and knaves their wine,
A man's a man for a' that.
For a' that, and a' that,
Their tinsel show, and a' that;
The honest man, tho' e'er sae poor,
Is King o' men for a' that.

Ye see yon birkie, ca'd a lord,
Wha struts, and stares, an' a' that;
Tho' hundreds worship at his word,
He's but a coof for a' that:
For a' that, and a' that,
His riband, star, and a' that,
The man of independent mind,
He looks and laughs at a' that.

A prince can mak a belted knight,
A marquis, duke, and a' that;
But an honest man's aboon his might,
Guid faith he mauna fa' that!
For a' that, and a' that;

133

Their dignities, and a' that;
The pith o' sense, and pride o' worth,
Are higher rank than a' that.

Then let us pray that come it may
As come it will for a' that,
That sense and worth o'er a' the earth,
Shall bear the gree an' a' that;
For a' that, and a' that,
It's comin' yet for a' that,
That man to man, the world o'er,
Shall brithers be for a' that.

Bettmann

Jest 'Fore Christmas

EUGENE FIELD
*(Born September 3, 1850;
died November 4, 1895)*

Father calls me William, sister calls me Will,
Mother calls me Willie, but the fellers call me Bill!
Mighty glad I ain't a girl—ruther be a boy,
Without them sashes, curls, an' things that's worn by Fauntleroy!
Love to chawnk green apples an' go swimmin' in the lake—
Hate to take the castor-ile they give for belly-ache!
'Most all the time, the whole year round, there ain't no flies on me,
But jest 'fore Christmas, I'm as good as I kin be!

Got a yeller dog named Sport, sick him on the cat;
First thing she knows she doesn't know where she is at!
Got a clipper sled, an' when us kids goes out to slide,
'Long comes the grocery cart, an' we all hook a ride!
But sometimes when the grocery man is worrited an' cross,
He reaches at us with his whip, an' larrups up his hoss,
An' then I laff an' holler, "Oh, ye never teched *me!*"
But jest 'fore Christmas I'm as good as I kin be!

Gran'ma says she hopes that when I git to be a man,
I'll be a missionarer like her oldest brother, Dan,
As was et up by the cannibals that live in Ceylon's Isle,
Where every prospeck pleases, an' only man is vile!
But gran'ma she has never been to see a Wild West show,
Nor read the life of Daniel Boone, or else I guess she'd know
That Buff'lo Bill an' cowboys is good enough for me!
Excep' jest 'fore Christmas, when I'm as good as I kin be!

And then old Sport he hangs around, so solemn-like an' still,
His eyes they seem a-sayin': "What's the matter, little Bill?"
The old cat sneaks down off her perch an' wonders what's become
Of them two enemies of hern that used to make things hum!
But I am so perlite an' tend so earnestly to biz,
That mother says to father: "How improved our Willie is!"
But father, havin' been a boy himself, suspicions me
When, jest 'fore Christmas, I'm as good as I kin be!

For Christmas, with its lots an' lots of candies, cakes an' toys,
Was made, they say, for proper kids an' not for naughty boys;
So wash yer face an' bresh yer hair, an' mind yer p's and q's,
And don't bust out yer pantaloons, and don't wear out yer shoes;
Say "Yessum" to the ladies, and "Yessur" to the men,
An' when they's company, don't pass yer plate for pie again;
But, thinkin' of the things yer'd like to see upon that tree,
Jest 'fore Christmas be as good as yer kin be!

From *The Poems of Eugene Field.* 1911. Published by Charles Scribner's Sons.

Bettmann

Gradatim

JOSIAH GILBERT HOLLAND
(Born July 24, 1819; died October 12, 1881)

Heaven is not gained at a single bound;
  But we build the ladder by which we rise
  From the lowly earth to the vaulted skies,
And we mount to its summit round by round.

I count this thing to be grandly true,
  That a noble deed is a step toward God—
  Lifting the soul from the common sod
To a purer air and a broader view.

We rise by things that are 'neath our feet;
  By what we have mastered of good and gain;
  By the pride deposed and the passion slain,
And the vanquished ills that we hourly meet.

We hope, we aspire, we resolve, we trust,
  When the morning calls us to life and light,
  But our hearts grow weary, and, ere the night,
Our lives are trailing the sordid dust.

We hope, we resolve, we aspire, we pray,
  And we think that we mount the air on wings
  Beyond the recall of sensual things,
While our feet still cling to the heavy clay.

Wings for the angels, but feet for men!
  We may borrow the wings to find the way—
  We may hope, and resolve, and aspire, and pray,
But our feet must rise, or we fall again.

Only in dreams is a ladder thrown
  From the weary earth to the sapphire walls;

136

But the dream departs, and the vision falls,
And the sleeper wakes on his pillow of stone.

Heaven is not reached at a single bound:
  But we build the ladder by which we rise
  From the lowly earth to the vaulted skies,
And we mount to its summit round by round.

From *Complete Political Writings* of J. G.
Holland. Copyright 1885.

Bettmann

The Barefoot Boy

JOHN GREENLEAF WHITTIER
*(Born December 17, 1807;
died September 7, 1892)*

Blessings on thee, little man,
Barefoot boy, with cheek of tan!
With thy turned-up pantaloons,
And thy merry whistled tunes;
With thy red lip, redder still,
Kissed by strawberries on the hill;
With the sunshine on thy face,
Through thy torn brim's jaunty grace,
From my heart I give thee joy,—
I was once a barefoot boy.
Prince thou art,—the grown-up man
Only is republican,
Let the million-dollared ride!
Barefoot, trudging at his side,
Thou hast more than he can buy,
In the reach of ear and eye—
Outward sunshine, inward joy;
Blessings on thee, barefoot boy!

Oh, for boyhood's painless play,
Sleep that wakes in laughing day,
Health that mocks the doctor's rules,

Knowledge never learned of schools,
Of the wild bee's morning chase,
Of the wild flower's time and place,
Flight of fowl and habitude
Of the tenants of the wood;
How the tortoise bears his shell,
How the woodchuck digs his cell,
And the groundmole sinks his well;
How the robin feeds her young,
How the oriole's nest is hung,
Where the whitest lilies blow,
Where the freshest berries grow,
Where the ground-nut trails its vine,
Where the wood-grape's clusters shine,
Of the black wasp's cunning way,—
Mason of his walls of clay,—
And the architectural plans
Of gray-hornet artisans!—
For, eschewing books and tasks,
Nature answers all he asks,
Hand in hand with her he walks,
Face to face with her he talks,
Part and parcel of her joy,—
Blessings on the barefoot boy!

Oh, for boyhood's time of June,
Crowding years in one brief moon,
When all things I heard or saw,
Me, their master, waited for.
I was rich in flowers and trees,
Humming-birds and honeybees,
For my sport the squirrel played,
Plied the snouted mole his spade;
For my task the blackberry cone
Purpled over hedge and stone;
Laughed the brook for my delight
Through the day and through the night,—
Whispering at the garden wall,
Talked with me from fall to fall;
Mine the sand-rimmed pickerel pond,
Mine the walnut slopes beyond,
Mine, on bending orchard trees,
Apples of Hesperides!
Still, as my horizon grew,
Larger grew my riches too;

All the world I saw or knew
Seemed a complex Chinese toy
Fashioned for a barefoot boy.

Oh, for festal dainties spread,
Like my bowl of milk and bread,—
Pewter spoon and bowl of wood,
On the doorstone, gray and rude!
O'er me, like a regal tent,
Cloudy-ribbed, the sunset bent,
Purple-curtained, fringed with gold,
Looped in many a wind-swung fold,
While for music came the play
Of the pied frog's orchestra,
And, to light the noisy choir,
Lit the fly his lamp of fire.
I was monarch; pomp and joy
Waited on thee, barefoot boy!

Cheerily, then, my little man,
Live and laugh as boyhood can!
Though the flinty slopes be hard,
Stubble-speared the new-mown sward,
Every morn shall lead thee through
Fresh baptisms of the dew;
Every evening from thy feet
Shall the cool wind kiss the heat;
All too soon these feet must hide
In the prison cells of pride,
Lose the freedom of the sod,
Like a colt's for work be shod,
Made to tread the mills of toil,
Up and down in ceaseless moil;
Happy if their track be found
Never on forbidden ground;
Happy if they sink not in
Quick and treacherous sands of sin,
Ah! that thou couldst know thy joy,
Ere it passes, barefoot boy!

The Flag Goes By

HENRY HOLCOMB BENNETT
(Born December 5, 1863; died April 30, 1924)

Hats off!
Along the street there comes
A blare of bugles, a ruffle of drums,
A flash of color beneath the sky:
    Hats off!
The flag is passing by!

Blue and crimson and white it shines,
Over the steel-tipped, ordered lines.
    Hats off!
The colors before us fly;
But more than the flag is passing by.

Sea-fights and land-fights, grim and great,
Fought to make and to save the State:
Weary marches and sinking ships;
Cheers of victory on dying lips;

Days of plenty and years of peace;
March of a strong land's swift increase;
Equal justice, right and law,
Stately honor and reverend awe;

Sign of a nation, great and strong
To ward her people from foreign wrong:
Pride and glory and honor,—all
Live in the colors to stand or fall.

    Hats off!
Along the street there comes
A blare of bugles, a ruffle of drums;
And loyal hearts are beating high:
    Hats off!
The flag is passing by!

Bettmann

Concord Hymn

Sung at the completion of the Battle Monument, April 19, 1886

RALPH WALDO EMERSON
(Born, May 25, 1803; died April 27, 1882)

By the rude bridge that arched the flood,
  Their flag to April's breeze unfurled,
Here once the embattled farmers stood,
  And fired the shot heard round the world.

The foe long since in silence slept;
  Alike the conqueror silent sleeps;
And Time the ruined bridge has swept
  Down the dark stream which seaward creeps.

On this green bank, by this soft stream,
  We set today a votive stone;
That memory may their deed redeem,
  When, like our sires, our sons are gone.

Spirit, that made those spirits dare
  To die, and leave their children free,
Bid Time and Nature gently spare
  The shaft we raise to them and thee.

Polonius' Advice to Laertes

From "Hamlet"

WILLIAM SHAKESPEARE
(Born April 23[?], 1564, died April 23, 1616)

There,—my blessing with you!
And these few precepts in thy memory
See thou character.—Give thy thoughts no tongue,
Nor any unproportion'd thought his act.
Be thou familiar, but by no means vulgar.
The friends thou hast, and their adoption tried,
Grapple them to thy soul with hoops of steel;
But do not dull thy palm with entertainment
Of each new-hatched, unfledged comrade. Beware
Of entrance to a quarrel; but being in,
Bear't that the opposed may beware of thee.
Give every man thine ear, but few thy voice:
Take each man's censure, but reserve thy judgment.
Costly thy habit as thy purse can buy,
But not expressed in fancy; rich, not gaudy:
For the apparel oft proclaims the man.
Neither a borrower nor a lender be,
For loan oft loses both itself and friend,
And borrowing dulls the edge of husbandry.
This above all: to thine own self be true,
And it must follow, as the night the day,
Thou canst not then be false to any man.

"The Things That Are More Excellent"

WILLIAM WATSON
(Born August 2, 1858; died 1935)

As we wax older on this earth,
    Till many a toy that charmed us seems
Emptied of beauty, stripped of worth,
    And mean as dust and dead as dreams,—
For gauds that perished, shows that passed,
    Some recompense the Fates have sent:
Thrice lovelier shine the things that last,
    The things that are more excellent.

Tired of the Senate's barren brawl,
    An hour with silence we prefer,
Where statelier rise the woods than all
    Yon towers of talk at Westminster.
Let this man prate and that man plot,
    On fame or place or title bent:
The votes of veering crowds are not
    The things that are more excellent.

Shall we perturb and vex our soul
    For "wrongs" which no true freedom mar,
Which no man's upright walk control,
    And from no guiltless deed debar?
What odds though tonguesters heal, or leave
    Unhealed, the grievance they invent?
To things, not phantoms, let us cleave—
    The things that are more excellent.

Nought nobler is, than to be free:
    The stars of heaven are free because
In amplitude of liberty
    Their joy is to obey the laws.
From servitude to freedom's *name*

Free thou thy mind in bondage pent;
Depose the fetich, and proclaim
   The things that are more excellent.

And in appropriate dust be hurled
   That dull, punctilious god, whom they
That call their tiny clan the world,
   Serve and obsequiously obey:
Who con their ritual of Routine.
   With minds to one dead likeness blent,
And never ev'n in dreams have seen
   The things that are more excellent.

To dress, to call, to dine, to break
   No canon of the social code,
The little laws that lacqueys make,
   The futile decalogue of Mode,—
How many a soul for these things lives,
   With pious passion, grave intent!
While Nature careless-handed gives
   The things that are more excellent.

To hug the wealth ye cannot use,
   And lack the riches all may gain,
O blind and wanting wit to choose,
   Who house the chaff and burn the grain!
And still doth life with starry towers
   Lure to the bright, divine ascent!—
Be yours the things ye would: be ours
   The things that are more excellent.

The grace of friendship—mind and heart
   Linked with their fellow heart and mind;
The gains of science, gifts of art;
   The sense of oneness with our kind;
The thirst to know and understand—
   A large and liberal discontent:
These are the goods in life's rich hand,
   The things that are more excellent.

In faultless rhythm the ocean rolls,
   A rapturous silence thrills the skies;
And on this earth are lovely souls,
   That softly look with aidful eyes.

Though dark, O God, Thy course and track,
    I think Thou must at least have meant
That nought which lives should wholly lack
    The things that are more excellent.

From *The Poems of William Watson.* Copyright by John Lane Co., Publishers, New York.

Life Sculpture

GEORGE WASHINGTON DOANE
(Born May 27, 1799; died April 27, 1859)

Courtesy *New England Magazine*

Chisel in hand stood a sculptor boy
    With his marble block before him,
And his eyes lit up with a smile of joy,
    As an angel-dream passed o'er him.

He carved the dream on that shapeless stone,
    With many a sharp incision;
With heaven's own light the sculpture shone,—
    He'd caught that angel-vision.

Children of life are we, as we stand
    With our lives uncarved before us,
Waiting the hour when, at God's command,
    Our life-dream shall pass o'er us.

If we carve it then on the yielding stone,
    With many a sharp incision,
Its heavenly beauty shall be our own,—
    Our lives, that angel-vision.

Keep a-Goin'

FRANK L. STANTON
(Born February 22, 1857; died January 7, 1927)

If you strike a thorn or rose,
    Keep a'goin'!
If it hails or if it snows,
    Keep a-goin'!
'Taint no use to sit an' whine
When the fish ain't on your line;
Bait your hook an' keep a-tryin'—
    Keep a-goin'!

When the weather kills your crop,
    Keep a-goin'!
Though 'tis work to reach the top,
    Keep a-goin'!
S'pose you're out o' ev'ry dime,
Gittin' broke ain't any crime;
Tell the world you're feelin' *prime*—
    Keep a-goin'!

When it looks like all is up,
    Keep a-goin'!
Drain the sweetness from the cup,
    Keep a-goin'!
See the wild birds on the wing,
Hear the bells that sweetly ring,
When you feel like surgin', sing—
    Keep a-goin'!

Bettmann

Marmion and Douglas

From "Marmion"

SIR WALTER SCOTT
(Born August 15, 1771; died September 21, 1832)

The train from out the castle drew,
But Marmion stopped to bid adieu:—
　　"Though something I might plain," he said
"Of cold respect to stranger guest,
Sent hither by your king's behest,
　　While in Tantallon's towers I stayed,
Part we in friendship from your land,
And noble Earl, receive my hand."—

But Douglas round him drew his cloak,
Folded his arms, and thus he spoke:—
"My manors, halls, and bowers shall still
Be open, at my sovereign's will
To each one whom he lists, howe'er
Unmeet to be the owner's peer.
My castles are my king's alone
From turret to foundation-stone,—
The hand of Douglas is his own;
And never shall in friendly grasp
The hand of such as Marmion clasp."—

Burned Marmion's swarthy cheek like fire,
And shook his very frame for ire,
　　And—"This to me!" he said,—
"An't were not for thy hoary beard,
Such hand as Marmion's had not spared
　　To cleave the Douglas' head!
And first I tell thee, haughty Peer,
He who does England's message here,
Although the meanest in her state,
May well, proud Angus, be thy mate:
And, Douglas, more I tell thee here,

147

Even in thy pitch of pride,
Here in thy hold, thy vassals near,
(Nay, never look upon your lord,
And lay your hands upon your sword,)
    I tell thee, thou'rt defied!
And if thou said'st I am not peer
To any lord in Scotland here,
Lowland or Highland, far or near,
    Lord Angus, thou hast lied!"—
On the Earl's cheek the flush of rage
O'ercame the ashen hue of age;
Fierce he broke forth,—"And dar'st thou then
To beard the lion in his den,
    The Douglas in his hall?
And hop'st thou hence unscathed to go?
No, by St. Bride of Bothwell, no!
Up drawbridge, grooms,—what, Warder, ho!
    Let the portcullis fall."—

Lord Marmion turned,—well was his need!—
And dashed the rowels in his steed,
Like arrow through the archway sprung;
The ponderous gate behind him rung:
To pass there was such scanty room,
The bars, descending, razed his plume.

The steed along the drawbridge flies,
Just as it trembled on the rise;
Not lighter does the swallow skim
Along the smooth lake's level brim;
And when Lord Marmion reached his band
He halts, and turns with clenchèd hand,
And shout of loud defiance pours,
And shook his gauntlet at the towers.

Bettmann

Ode on a Grecian Urn

John Keats
(Born October 31, 1795; died February 23, 1821)

Thou still unravished bride of quietness,
  Thou foster child of Silence and slow Time,
Sylvan historian, who canst thus express
  A flowery tale more sweetly than our rhyme:
What leaf-fring'd legend haunts about thy shape
  Of deities or mortals, or of both,
    In Tempe or the dales of Arcady?
What men or gods are these? What maidens loath?
  What mad pursuit? What struggle to escape?
    What pipes and timbrels? What wild ecstasy?

Heard melodies are sweet, but those unheard
  Are sweeter; therefore, ye soft pipes, play on;
Not to the sensual ear, but more endeared,
  Pipe to the spirit ditties of no tone;
Fair youth, beneath the trees, thou canst not leave
  Thy song, nor ever can those trees be bare;
    Bold Lover, never, never canst thou kiss,
Though winning near the goal—yet, do not grieve;
  She cannot fade, though thou hast not thy bliss,
    For ever wilt thou love, and she be fair!

Ah, happy, happy boughs! that cannot shed
  Your leaves, nor ever bid the Spring adieu;
And, happy melodist, unwearied,
  For ever piping songs for ever new;
More happy love! more happy, happy love!
  For ever warm and still to be enjoy'd,
    For ever panting, and for ever young;
All breathing human passion far above,
  That leaves a heart high-sorrowful and cloy'd,
    A burning forehead, and a parching tongue.

Who are these coming to the sacrifice?
To what green altar, O mysterious priest,
Lead'st thou that heifer lowing at the skies,
And all her silken flanks with garlands drest?
What little town by river or seashore,
Or mountain-built with peaceful citadel,
Is emptied of this folk, this pious morn?
And, little town, thy streets for evermore
Will silent be; and not a soul to tell
Why thou are desolate, can e'er return.

O Attic shape! Fair attitude! with brede
Of marble men and maidens overwrought,
With forest branches and the trodden weed;
Thou, silent form, dost tease us out of thought
As doth eternity: Cold Pastoral!
When old age shall this generation waste,
Thou shalt remain, in midst of other woe
Than ours, a friend to man, to whom thou say'st,
"Beauty is truth, truth beauty,"—that is all
Ye know on earth, and all ye need to know.

Bettmann

The Choir Invisible

GEORGE ELIOT (MARY ANN EVANS)
*(Born November 22, 1819;
died December 22, 1880)*

Oh, may I join the choir invisible
Of those immortal dead who live again
In minds made better by their presence; live
In pulses stirred to generosity,
In deeds of daring rectitude, in scorn
For miserable aims that end with self,
In thoughts sublime that pierce the night like stars,
And with their mild persistence urge men's search

To vaster issues. So to live is heaven:
To make undying music in the world,
Breathing a beauteous order that controls
With growing sway the growing life of man.
So we inherit that sweet purity
For which we struggled, failed, and agonized
With widening retrospect that bred despair.
Rebellious flesh that would not be subdued,
A vicious parent shaming still its child,
Poor anxious penitence, is quick dissolved;
Its discords, quenched by meeting harmonies,
Die in the large and charitable air.
And all our rarer, better, truer self,
That sobbed religiously in yearning song,
That watched to ease the burden of the world,
Laboriously tracing what must be,
And what may yet be better,—saw within
A worthier image for the sanctuary,
And shaped it forth before the multitude,
Divinely human, raising worship so
To higher reverence more mixed with love,—
That better self shall live till human Time
Shall fold its eyelids, and the human sky
Be gathered like a scroll within the tomb
Unread forever. This is life to come,—
Which martyred men have made more glorious
For us who strive to follow. May I reach
That purest heaven,—be to other souls
The cup of strength in some great agony,
Enkindle generous ardor, feed pure love,
Beget the smiles that have no cruelty,
Be the sweet presence of a good diffused,
And in diffusion ever more intense!
So shall I join the choir invisible
Whose music is the gladness of the world.

The Heart of the Tree

HENRY CUYLER BUNNER
(Born August 3, 1855; died May 11, 1896)

What does he plant who plants a tree?
  He plants a friend of sun and sky;
 He plants the flag of breezes free;
The shaft of beauty, towering high;
He plants a home to heaven anigh
  For song and mother-croon of bird
  In hushed and happy twilight heard—
The treble of heaven's harmony—
These things he plants who plants a tree.

What does he plant who plants a tree?
  He plants cool shade and tender rain,
 And seed and bud of days to be,
And years that fade and flush again;
He plants the glory of the plain;
  He plants the forest's heritage;
  The harvest of a coming age;
The joy that unborn eyes shall see—
These things he plants who plants a tree.

What does he plant who plants a tree?
  He plants, in sap and leaf and wood,
 In love of home and loyalty
And far-cast thought of civic good—
His blessings on the neighborhood
  Who in the hollow of His hand
  Holds all the growth of all our land—
A nation's growth from sea to sea
Stirs in his heart who plants a tree.

By special arrangement with Charles Scribner's Sons, Publishers.

Bettmann

Soliloquy from "Hamlet"

WILLIAM SHAKESPEARE
(Born April 23[?], 1564; died April 23, 1616)

To be, or not to be; that is the question;
Whether 'tis nobler in the mind to suffer
The slings and arrows of outrageous fortune,
Or to take arms against a sea of troubles,
And by opposing end them. To die: to sleep:
No more; and by a sleep to say we end
The heart-ache and the thousand natural shocks
That flesh is heir to; 'tis a consummation
Devoutly to be wished. To die; to sleep;
To sleep: perchance to dream: aye, there's the rub;
For in that sleep of death what dreams may come,
When we have shuffled off this mortal coil,
Must give us pause: there's the respect
That makes calamity of so long life;
For who would bear the whips and scorns of time,
The oppressor's wrong, the proud man's contumely,
The pangs of despis'd love, the law's delay,
The insolence of office, and the spurns
That patient merit of the unworthy takes,
When he himself might his quietus make
With a bare bodkin? Who would fardels bear,
To grunt and sweat under a weary life,
But that the dread of something after death—
The undiscover'd country from whose bourn
No traveler returns—puzzles the will
And makes us rather bear those ills we have
Than fly to others that we know not of?
Thus conscience does make cowards of us all,
And thus the native hue of resolution
Is sicklied o'er with the pale cast of thought,
And enterprises of great pith and moment
With this regard their currents turn awry,
And lose the name of action.

Bettmann

She Was a Phantom of Delight

WILLIAM WORDSWORTH
(Born April 7, 1770; died April 23, 1850)

She was a phantom of delight
When first she gleamed upon my sight;
A lovely apparition, sent
To be a moment's ornament;
Her eyes as stars of twilight fair;
Like twilight's, too, her dusky hair;
But all things else about her drawn
From May-time and the cheerful dawn;
A dancing shape, an image gay,
To haunt, to startle, and waylay.

I saw her upon nearer view,
A spirit, yet a woman too!
Her household motions light and free,
And step of virgin liberty;
A countenance in which did meet
Sweet records, promises as sweet;
A creature not too bright or good
For human nature's daily food,
For transient sorrows, simple wiles,
Praise, blame, love, kisses, tears, and smiles.

And now I see with eye serene
The very pulse of the machine;
A being breathing thoughtful breath,
A traveler between life and death;
The reason firm, the temperate will,
Endurance, foresight, strength, and skill;
A perfect woman, nobly planned
To warn, to comfort, and command;
And yet a spirit still, and bright
With something of angelic light.

Bettmann

The Spider and the Fly
A Fable

MARY HOWITT
(Born March 12, 1799; died January 30, 1888)

"Will you walk into my parlor?" said the spider to the fly;
" 'Tis the prettiest little parlor that ever you did spy.
The way into my parlor is up a winding stair,
And I have many pretty things to show when you are there."
"O no, no," said the little fly, "to ask me is in vain,
For who goes up your winding stair can ne'er come down again."

"I'm sure you must be weary, dear, with soaring up so high;
Will you rest upon my little bed?" said the spider to the fly.
"There are pretty curtains drawn around, the sheets are fine and
    thin,
And if you like to rest awhile, I'll snugly tuck you in."
"O no, no," said the little fly, "for I've often heard it said,
They *never, never wake* again, who sleep upon *your* bed."

Said the cunning spider to the fly, "Dear friend, what shall I do,
To prove the warm affection I've always felt for you?
I have within my pantry good store of all that's nice;
I'm sure you're very welcome; will you please to take a slice?"
"O no, no," said the little fly, "kind sir, that cannot be;
I've heard what's in your pantry, and I do not wish to see."

"Sweet creature!" said the spider, "You're witty and you're wise,
How handsome are your gauzy wings, how brilliant are your eyes!
I have a little looking-glass upon my parlor shelf,
If you'll step in one moment, dear, you shall behold yourself."
"I thank you, gentle sir,' she said, "for what you're pleased to say,
And bidding you good-morning *now*, I'll call *another* day."

The spider turned him round about, and went into his den,
For well he knew the silly fly would soon be back again:
So he wove a subtle web, in a little corner sly,

And set his table ready to dine upon the fly.
Then he came out to his door again, and merrily did sing,
"Come hither, hither, pretty fly, with the pearl and silver wing:
Your robes are green and purple; there's a crest upon your head;
Your eyes are like the diamond bright, but mine are dull as lead."

Alas, alas! how very soon this silly little fly,
Hearing his wily flattering words, came slowly flitting by.
With buzzing wings she hung aloft, then near and nearer drew,
Thinking only of her brilliant eyes, and green and purple hue;
Thinking only of her crested head—*poor foolish thing!* At last,
Up jumped the cunning spider, and fiercely held her fast.
He dragged her up his winding stair, into his dismal den,
Within his little parlor; but she ne'er came out again!

And now, dear little children, who may this story read,
To idle, silly, flattering words, I pray you ne'er give heed;
Unto an evil counselor close heart, and ear, and eye,
And take a lesson from this tale of the Spider and the Fly.

Bettmann

Maud Muller

JOHN GREENLEAF WHITTIER
*(Born December 17, 1807;
died September 7, 1892)*

Maud Muller, on a summer's day,
Raked the meadow sweet with hay.
Beneath her torn hat glowed the wealth
Of simple beauty and rustic health.
Singing, she wrought, and her merry glee
The mock-bird echoed from his tree.

But when she glanced to the far-off town,
White from its hill-slope looking down,
The sweet song died, and a vague unrest

And a nameless longing filled her breast;
A wish, that she hardly dared to own,
For something better than she had known.

The Judge rode slowly down the lane,
Smoothing his horse's chestnut mane:
He drew his bridle in the shade
Of the apple-trees, to greet the maid,
And asked a draught from the spring that flowed
Through the meadow across the road.

She stooped where the cool spring bubbled up,
And filled for him her small tin cup,
And blushed as she gave it, looking down
On her feet so bare, and her tattered gown.
"Thanks!" said the Judge, "a sweeter draught
From a fairer hand was never quaffed."

He spoke of the grass, and flowers, and trees,
Of the singing birds and the humming bees;
Then talked of the haying, and wondered whether
The cloud in the west would bring foul weather.
And Maud forgot her brier-torn gown,
And her graceful ankles bare and brown,
And listened, while a pleased surprise
Looked from her long-lashed hazel eyes.

At last, like one who for delay
Seeks a vain excuse, he rode away.
Maud Muller looked and sighed: "Ah, me!
That I the Judge's bride might be!
He would dress me up in silks so fine,
And praise and toast me at his wine.

"My father should wear a broadcloth coat;
My brother should sail a painted boat;
I'd dress my mother so grand and gay,
And the baby should have a new toy each day;
And I'd feed the hungry and clothe the poor,
And all should bless me who left our door."

The Judge looked back as he climbed the hill,
And saw Maud Muller standing still.
"A form more fair, a face more sweet,
Ne'er has it been my lot to meet;

And her modest answer and graceful air
Show her wise and good as she is fair.

"Would she were mine, and I to-day,
Like her, a harvester of hay;
No doubtful balance of rights and wrongs,
Nor weary lawyers with endless tongues;
But low of cattle and song of birds,
And health, and quiet, and loving words."

But he thought of his sisters, proud and cold,
And his mother, vain of her rank and gold;
So, closing his heart, the Judge rode on,
And Maud was left in the field alone.
But the lawyers smiled that afternoon,
When he hummed in court an old love-tune;
And the young girl mused beside the well,
Till the rain on the unraked clover fell.

He wedded a wife of richest dower,
Who lived for fashion, as he for power;
Yet oft, in his marble hearth's bright glow,
He watched a picture come and go;
And sweet Maud Muller's hazel eyes,
Looked out in their innocent surprise.

Oft when the wine in his glass was red,
He longed for the wayside well instead;
And closed his eyes on his garnished rooms,
To dream of meadows and clover-blooms.
And the proud man sighed, with a secret pain,
"Ah, that I were free again!
Free as when I rode that day,
Where the barefoot maiden raked her hay."

She wedded a man unlearned and poor,
And many children played round her door;
But care and sorrow and wasting pain
Left their traces on heart and brain.
And oft when the summer sun shone hot
On the new-mown hay in the meadow lot,
And she heard the little spring brook fall
Over the roadside, through the wall,
In the shade of the apple-tree again
She saw a rider draw his rein,

And, gazing down with timid grace,
She felt his pleased eyes read her face.

Sometimes her narrow kitchen walls
Stretched away into stately halls;
The weary wheel to a spinet turned;
The tallow candle an astral burned;
And for him who sat by the chimney lug,
Dozing and grumbling o'er pipe and mug,
A manly form at her side she saw,
And joy was duty, and love was law.
Then she took up her burden of life again,
Saying only, "It might have been!"

Alas for maiden, alas for Judge,
For rich repiner and household drudge!
God pity them both! and pity us all,
Who vainly the dreams of youth recall;
For of all sad words of tongue or pen
The saddest are these: "It might have been!"
Ah, well! for us all some sweet hope lies
Deeply buried from human eyes;
And in the hereafter angels may
Roll the stone from its grave away!

The Night Before Christmas

CLEMENT CLARKE MOORE
(Born July 15, 1779; died July 10, 1863)

Bettmann

'Twas the night before Christmas, when all through the house
Not a creature was stirring, not even a mouse;
The stockings were hung by the chimney with care,
In hopes that St. Nicholas soon would be there;
The children were nestled all snug in their beds,
While visions of sugar-plums danced in their heads;
And Mamma in her kerchief, and I in my cap,
Had just settled our brains for a long winter's nap,
When out on the lawn there arose such a clatter,
I sprang from my bed to see what was the matter.
Away to the window I flew like a flash,
Tore open the shutters and threw up the sash.
The moon, on the breast of the new-fallen snow,
Gave a luster of mid-day to objects below;
When, what to my wondering eyes should appear,
But a miniature sleigh, and eight tiny reindeer,
With a little old driver, so lively and quick,
I knew in a moment it must be St. Nick.
More rapid than eagles his coursers they came,
And he whistled, and shouted, and called them by name:
"Now, Dasher! now, Dancer! now, Prancer and Vixen!
On, Comet! on, Cupid! on, Donder and Blitzen!
To the top of the porch, to the top of the wall!
Now, dash away, dash away, dash away, all!"
As dry leaves that before the wild hurricane fly,
When they meet with an obstacle, mount to the sky,
So, up to the house-top the coursers they flew,
With the sleigh full of toys—and St. Nicholas, too.
And then in a twinkling I heard on the roof
The prancing and pawing of each little hoof.
As I drew in my head, and was turning around,
Down the chimney St. Nicholas came with a bound.

He was dressed all in fur from his head to his foot,
And his clothes were all tarnished with ashes and soot;
A bundle of toys he had flung on his back,
And he looked like a peddler just opening his pack.
His eyes how they twinkled! his dimples how merry!
His cheeks were like roses, his nose like a cherry;
His droll little mouth was drawn up like a bow,
And the beard on his chin was as white as the snow.
The stump of a pipe he held tight in his teeth,
And the smoke it encircled his head like a wreath;
He had a broad face and a little round belly
That shook, when he laughed, like a bowlful of jelly.
He was chubby and plump—a right jolly old elf;
And I laughed when I saw him, in spite of myself.
A wink of his eye, and a twist of his head,
Soon gave me to know I had nothing to dread.
He spoke not a word, but went straight to his work,
And filled all the stockings; then turned with a jerk,
And laying his finger aside of his nose,
And giving a nod, up the chimney he rose.
He sprang to his sleigh, to his team gave a whistle,
And away they all flew like the down of a thistle;
But I heard him exclaim, ere he drove out of sight,
"Happy Christmas to all, and to all a goodnight!"

Bettmann

Crossing the Bar

ALFRED TENNYSON
(First Baron)
(Born August 6, 1809; Died October 6, 1892)

Sunset and evening star,
    And one clear call for me,
And may there be no moaning of the bar,
    When I put out to sea.

But such a tide as moving seems asleep,
    Too full for sound and foam,

161

When that which drew from out the boundless deep
  Turns again home.

Twilight and evening bell,
  And after that the dark!
And may there be no sadness of farewell,
  When I embark;

For tho' from out our bourne of time and place
  The flood may bear me far,
I hope to see my Pilot face to face
  When I have crossed the bar.

Home

EDGAR A. GUEST

(Born August 20, 1881; died August 5, 1959)

It takes a heap o' livin' in a house t' make it home,
A heap o' sun an' shadder, an' ye sometimes have t' roam
Afore ye really 'preciate the things ye lef' behind,
An' hunger fer 'em somehow, with 'em allus on yer mind.
It don't make any differunce how rich ye get t' be,
How much yer chairs an' tables cost, how great yer luxury;
It ain't home t' ye, though it be the palace of a king,
Until somehow yer soul is sort o' wrapped 'round everything.

Home ain't a place that gold can buy or get up in a minute;
Afore it's home there's got t' be a heap o' livin' in it;
Within the walls there's got t' be some babies born, and then
Right there ye've got t' bring 'em up t' women good, an' men;
And gradjerly, as time goes on, ye find ye wouldn't part
With anything they ever used—they're grown into yer heart:
The old high chairs, the playthings, too, the little shoes they wore
Ye hoard; an' if ye could ye'd keep the thumbmarks on the door.

Ye've got t' weep t' make it home, ye've got t' sit an' sigh.
An' watch beside a loved one's bed, an' know that Death is nigh;
An' in the stillness o' the night t' see Death's angel come,
An' close the eyes o' her that smiled, an' leave her sweet voice dumb.
Fer these are scenes that grip the heart, an' when yer tears are dried,
Ye find the home is dearer than it was, an' sanctified;
An' tuggin' at ye always are the pleasant memories
O' her that was an' is no more—ye can't escape from these.

Ye've got t' sing an' dance fer years, ye've got t' romp an' play,
An' learn t' love the things ye have by usin' 'em each day;
Even the roses 'round the porch must blossom year by year
Afore they 'come a part o' ye, suggestin' someone dear
Who used t' love 'em long ago, an' trained 'em jes' t' run
The way they do, so's they would get the early mornin' sun;
Ye've got t' love each brick an' stone from cellar up t' dome:
It takes a heap o' livin' in a house t' make it home.

Reprinted from *A Heap o' Livin'* by Edgar A. Guest. Copyright 1916.

Bettmann

My Kate

ELIZABETH BARRETT BROWNING
(Born March 6, 1806; died June 29, 1861)

She was not as pretty as women I know,
And yet all your best made of sunshine and snow
Drop to shade, melt to nought in the long-trodden ways,
While she's still remembered on warm and cold days—
        My Kate.

Her air had a meaning, her movements a grace;
You turned from the fairest to gaze on her face;
And when you had once seen her forehead and mouth,
You saw as distinctly her soul and her truth—
        My Kate.

Such a blue inner light from her eyelids outbroke,
You looked at her silence and fancied she spoke;
When she did, so peculiar yet soft was the tone,
Though the loudest spoke also, you heard her alone—
                                        My Kate.

I doubt if she said to you much that could act
As a thought or suggestion; she did not attract
In the sense of the brilliant or wise; I infer
'Twas her thinking of others made you think of her—
                                        My Kate.

She never found fault with you, never implied
Your wrong by her right; and yet men at her side
Grew nobler, girls purer, as through the whole town
The children were gladder that pulled at her gown—
                                        My Kate.

None knelt at her feet confessed lovers in thrall;
They knelt more to God than they used—that was all;
If you praised her as charming, some asked what you meant,
But the charm of her presence was felt when she went—
                                        My Kate.

The weak and the gentle, the ribald and rude,
She took as she found them, and did them all good;
It always was so with her—see what you have!
She has made the grass greener even here with her grave—
                                        My Kate.

Bettmann

Lincoln,
the Man of the People

Edwin Markham

*(Born Oregon City, Oregon, 1852;
died March 7, 1940)*

When the Norn Mother saw the Whirlwind Hour
Greatening and darkening as it hurried on,
She left the Heaven of Heroes and came down
To make a man to meet the mortal need.
She took the tried clay of the common road—
Clay warm yet with the genial heat of Earth,
Dasht through it all a strain of prophecy;
Tempered the heap with thrill of human tears;
Then mixt a laughter with the serious stuff.
Into the shape she breathed a flame to light
That tender, tragic, ever-changing face;
And laid on him a sense of the Mystic Powers,
Moving—all husht—behind the mortal veil.
Here was a man to hold against the world,
A man to match the mountains and the sea.

The color of the ground was in him, the red earth;
The smack and tang of elemental things:
The rectitude and patience of the cliff;
The good-will of the rain that loves all leaves;
The friendly welcome of the wayside well;
The courage of the bird that dares the sea;
The gladness of the wind that shakes the corn;
The pity of the snow that hides all scars;
The secrecy of streams that make their way
Under the mountain to the rifted rock;
The tolerance and equity of light
That gives as freely to the shrinking flower
As to the great oak flaring to the wind—
To the grave's low hill as to the Matterhorn
That shoulders out the sky. Sprung from the West,
He drank the valorous youth of a new world.

165

The strength of virgin forests braced his mind,
The hush of spacious prairies stilled his soul.
His words were oaks in acorns; and his thoughts
Were roots that firmly gript the granite truth.

Up from log cabin to the Capitol,
One fire was on his spirit, one resolve—
To send the keen ax to the root of wrong,
Clearing a free way for the feet of God,
The eyes of conscience testing every stroke,
To make his deed the measure of a man.
He built the rail-pile as he built the State,
Pouring his splendid strength through every blow:
The grip that swung the ax in Illinois
Was on the pen that set a people free.

So came the Captain with the mighty heart;
And when the judgment thunders split the house,
Wrenching the rafters from their ancient rest,
He held the ridgepole up, and spikt again
The rafters of the Home. He held his place—
Held the long purpose like a growing tree—
Held on through blame and faltered not at praise.
And when he fell in whirlwind, he went down
As when a lordly cedar, green with boughs,
Goes down with a great shout upon the hills,
And leaves a lonesome place against the sky.

This revised version was chosen out of 250 Lincoln poems by the committee headed by Chief Justice Taft to be read at the dedication of the great Lincoln Memorial erected by the Government in Washington, D.C. This was in 1922. There were 100,000 listeners on the ground and two million over the radio. President Harding delivered the address, and Edwin Markham read the poem. It is taken from his volume, *Lincoln and Other Poems*, published by Doubleday, Page and Company— copyrighted 1900, by the author, and used by his permission.

Bettmann

On the Building of Springfield

VACHEL LINDSAY

*(Born Springfield, Ill., November 10, 1879;
died December 5, 1931)*

Let not our town be large, remembering
    That little Athens was the Muses' home,
That Oxford rules the heart of London still,
    That Florence gave the Renaissance to Rome.

Record it for the grandson of your son—
    A city is not builded in a day:
Our little town cannot complete her soul
    Till countless generations pass away.

Now let each child be joined as to a church
    To her perpetual hopes, each man ordained:
Let every street be made a reverent aisle
    Where Music grows and Beauty is unchained.

Let Science and Machinery and Trade
    Be slaves of her, and make her all in all,
Building against our blatant, restless time
    An unseen, skilful, medieval wall.

Let every citizen be rich toward God.
    Let Christ, the beggar, teach divinity.
Let no man rule who holds his money dear.
    Let this, our city, be our luxury.

We should build parks that students from afar
    Would choose to starve in, rather than go home,
Fair little squares, with Phidian ornament.
    Food for the spirit, milk and honeycomb.

Songs shall be sung by us in that good day,
    Songs we have written, blood within the rhyme

167

Beating, as when Old England still was glad,—
  The purple, rich Elizabethan time.

*   *   *   *

Say, is my prophecy too fair and far?
  I only know, unless her faith be high,
The soul of this, our Nineveh, is doomed,
  Our little Babylon will surely die.

Some city on the breast of Illinois
  No wiser and no better at the start
By faith shall rise redeemed, by faith shall rise
  Bearing the western glory in her heart.

The genius of the Maple, Elm and Oak,
  The secret hidden in each grain of corn,
The glory that the prairie angels sing
  At night when sons of Life and Love are born,

Born but to struggle, squalid and alone,
  Broken and wandering in their early years;
When will they make our dusty streets their goal,
  Within our attics hide their sacred tears?

When will they start our vulgar blood athrill
  With living language, words that set us free?
When will they make a path of beauty clear
  Between our riches and our liberty?

We must have many Lincoln-hearted men—
  A city is not builded in a day—
And they must do their work, and come and go
  While countless generations pass away.

From *Collected Poems* by Vachel Lindsay and published by The Macmillan Co. Copyright 1923. By permission of the author and publisher.

Mending Wall

ROBERT FROST

*(Born San Francisco, March 26, 1875;
died January 29, 1963)*

Something there is that doesn't love a wall,
That sends the frozen-ground-swell under it,
And spills the upper boulders in the sun;
And makes gaps even two can pass abreast.
The work of hunters is another thing:
I have come after them and made repair
Where they have left not one stone on a stone,
But they would have the rabbit out of hiding,
To please the yelping dogs. The gaps I mean,
No one has seen them made or heard them made,
But at spring mending-time we find them there.
I let my neighbour know beyond the hill;
And on a day we meet to walk the line
And set the wall between us once again.
We keep the wall between us as we go.
To each the boulders that have fallen to each.
And some are loaves and some so nearly balls
We have to use a spell to make them balance:
"Stay where you are until our backs are turned!"
We wear our fingers rough with handling them.
Oh, just another kind of out-door game,
One on a a side. It comes to little more:
There where it is we do not need the wall:
He is all pine and I am apple orchard.
My apple trees will never get across
And eat the cones under his pines, I tell him.
He only says, "Good fences make good neighbours."
Spring is the mischief in me, and I wonder
If I could put a notion in his head:
"*Why* do they make good neighbours? Isn't it
Where there are cows? But here there are no cows.
Before I built a wall I'd ask to know

What I was walling in or walling out,
And to whom I was like to give offense.
Something there is that doesn't love a wall,
That wants it down." I could say "Elves" to him,
But it's not elves exactly, and I'd rather
He said it for himself. I see him there
Bringing a stone grasped firmly by the top
In each hand, like an old-stone savage armed.
He moves in darkness as it seems to me,
Not of woods only and the shade of trees.
He will not go behind his father's saying,
And he likes having thought of it so well
He says again, "Good fences make good neighbours."

From *North of Boston,* by Robert Frost. Copyright 1915. Published by Henry Holt & Co. Special permission of the publisher.

Bettmann

The Fool's Prayer

EDWARD R. SILL
(Born April 29, 1841; died February 27, 1887)

The royal feast was done; the King
   Sought some new sport to banish care,
And to his jester cried: "Sir Fool,
   Kneel now, and make for us a prayer!"

The jester doffed his cap and bells,
   And stood the mocking court before;
They could not see the bitter smile
   Behind the painted grin he wore.

He bowed his head, and bent his knee
   Upon the monarch's silken stool;
His pleading voice arose: "O Lord,
   Be merciful to me, a fool!

"No pity, Lord, could change the heart
   From red with wrong to white as wool;
The rod must heal the sin: but, Lord,
   Be merciful to me, a fool!

" 'Tis not by guilt the onward sweep
   Of truth and right, O Lord, we stay;
'Tis by our follies that so long
   We hold the earth from heaven away.

"These clumsy feet, still in the mire,
   Go crushing blossoms without end;
These hard, well-meaning hands we thrust
   Among the heart-strings of a friend.

"The ill-timed truth we might have kept—
   Who knows how sharp it pierced and stung?
The word we had not sense to say—
   Who knows how grandly it had rung?

"Our faults no tenderness should ask,
   The chastening stripes must cleanse them all;
But for our blunders—oh, in shame
   Before the eyes of heaven we fall.

"Earth bears no balsam for mistakes;
   Men crown the knave, and scourge the tool
That did his will; but Thou, O Lord,
   Be merciful to me, a fool!"

The room was hushed; in silence rose
   The King, and sought his gardens cool,
And walked apart, and murmured low,
   "Be merciful to me, a fool!"

Bettmann

To a Waterfowl

WILLIAM CULLEN BRYANT
(Born November 3, 1794; died June 12, 1878)

Whither, 'midst falling dew,
    While glow the heavens with the last steps of day,
Far, through their rosy depths, dost thou pursue
    Thy solitary way?

Vainly the fowler's eye
    Might mark thy distant flight to do thee wrong,
As, darkly painted on the crimson sky,
    Thy figure floats along.

Seek'st thou the plashy brink
    Of weedy lake, or marge of river wide,
Or where the rocking billows rise and sink
    On the chafed ocean's side?

There is a Power whose care
    Teaches thy way along that pathless coast—
The desert and illimitable air—
    Lone wandering, but not lost.

All day thy wings have fanned,
    At that far height, the cold, thin atmosphere,
Yet stoop not weary, to the welcome land,
    Though the dark night is near.

And soon that toil shall end;
    Soon shalt thou find a summer home, and rest,
And scream among thy fellows; reeds shall bend,
    Soon, o'er thy sheltered nest.

Thou'rt gone! the abyss of heaven
    Hath swallowed up thy form; yet on my heart

Deeply hath sunk the lesson thou has given,
  And shall not soon depart.

He who, from zone to zone,
  Guides through the boundless sky thy certain flight,
In the long way that I must tread alone
  Will lead my steps aright.

I Shall Not Pass This Way Again

A Symphony

EVA ROSE YORK
(Born December 22, 1858)

I shall not pass this way again—
  Although it bordered be with flowers,
  Although I rest in fragrant bowers,
    And hear the singing
    Of song-birds winging
To highest heaven their gladsome flight;
Though moons are full and stars are bright,
And winds and waves are softly sighing,
While leafy trees make low replying;
Though voices clear in joyous strain
Repeat a jubilant refrain;
Though rising suns their radiance throw
On summer's green and winter's snow,
In such rare splendor that my heart
Would ache from scenes like these to part;
    Though beauties heighten,
    And life-lights brighten,
And joys proceed from every pain,—
I shall not pass this way again.

Then let me pluck the flowers that blow,
And let me listen as I go
    To music rare

That fills the air;
And let hereafter
Songs and laughter
Fill every pause along the way;
And to my spirit let me say:
"O soul, be happy; soon 'tis trod,
The path made thus for thee by God.
Be happy thou, and bless His name
By whom such marvellous beauty came."
And let no chance by me be lost
To kindness show at any cost.
I shall not pass this way again;
Then let me now relieve some pain,
Remove some barrier from the road,
Or brighten some one's heavy load;
A helping hand to this one lend,
Then turn some other to befriend.

O God, forgive
That now I live
As if I might, sometime, return
To bless the weary ones that yearn
For help and comfort every day,—
For there be such along the way.
O God, forgive that I have seen
The beauty only, have not been
Awake to sorrow such as this;
That I have drunk the cup of bliss
Remembering not that those there be
Who drink the dregs of misery.

I love the beauty of the scene,
Would roam again o'er fields so green;
But since I may not, let me spend
My strength for others to the end,—
For those who tread on rock and stone,
And bear their burdens all alone,
Who loiter not in leafy bowers,
Nor hear the birds nor pluck the flowers.
A larger kindness give to me,
A deeper love and sympathy;
Then, O, one day
May someone say—
Remembering a lessened pain—
"Would she could pass this way again."

Taken by permission from *A Treasury of Canadian Verse*. Published by E. P. Dutton & Co.

Apostrophe to the Ocean

From "Childe Harold's Pilgrimage"

GEORGE GORDON BYRON
(Sixth Lord)
(Born January 22, 1788; died April 19, 1824)

Bettmann

There is a pleasure in the pathless woods,
   There is a rapture on the lonely shore,
There is society where none intrudes,
   By the deep sea, and music in its roar.
   I love not man the less, but Nature more,
From these our interviews, in which I steal
   From all I may be, or have been before,
To mingle with the universe, and feel
What I can ne'er express, yet can not all conceal.

Roll on, thou deep and dark blue ocean, roll!
   Ten thousand fleets sweep over thee in vain;
Man marks the earth with ruin, his control
   Stops with the shore; upon the watery plain
   The wrecks are all thy deed, nor doth remain
A shadow of man's ravage, save his own,
   When for a moment, like a drop of rain,
He sinks into thy depths with bubbling groan,
Without a grave, unknelled, uncoffined, and unknown.

His steps are not upon thy paths, thy fields
   Are not a spoil for him,—thou dost arise
And shake him from thee; the vile strength he wields
   For earth's destruction thou dost all despise,
   Spurning him from thy bosom to the skies,
And send'st him, shivering in thy playful spray
   And howling, to his gods, where haply lies
His pretty hope in some near port or bay,
And dashest him again to earth:—there let him lay.

The armaments which thunder-strike the walls
   Of rock-built cities, bidding nations quake,

And monarchs tremble in their capitals;
   The oak leviathans, whose huge ribs make
   Their clay creator the vain title take
Of lord of thee, and arbiter of war;—
   These are thy toys, and, as the snowy flake,
They melt into the nest of waves, which mar
Alike the Armada's pride or spoils of Trafalgar.

Thy shores are empires, changed in all save thee;
   Assyria, Greece, Rome, Carthage—what are they?
Thy waters wasted them while they were free,
   And many a tyrant since; their shores obey
   The stranger, slave, or savage; their decay
Has dried up realms to deserts: not so thou,
   Unchangeable save to thy wild waves' play;
Time writes no wrinkle on thy azure brow;
Such as creation's dawn beheld, thou rollest now.

Thou glorious mirror, where the Almighty's form
   Glasses itself in tempests; in all time,
Calm or convulsed; in breeze, or gale, or storm,
   Icing the pole, or in the torrid clime,
   Dark-heaving; boundless, endless, and sublime;—
The image of Eternity, the throne
   Of the Invisible; even from out thy slime
The monsters of the deep are made; each zone
Obeys thee; thou goest forth, dread, fathomless, alone.

And I have loved thee, Ocean! and my joy
   Of youthful sports was on thy breast to be
Borne, like thy bubbles, onward: from a boy
   I wanton'd with thy breakers—they to me
   Were a delight; and if the freshening sea
Made them a terror—'twas a pleasing fear,
   For I was as it were a child of thee,
And trusted to thy billows far and near,
And laid my hand upon thy mane—as I do here.

Bettmann

Renascence

EDNA ST. VINCENT MILLAY
(Born February 22, 1892; died October 19, 1950)

All I could see from where I stood
Was three long mountains and a wood;
I turned and looked the other way,
And saw three islands in a bay.
So with my eyes I traced the line
Of the horizon, thin and fine,
Straight around till I was come
Back to where I'd started from;
And all I saw from where I stood
Was three long mountains and a wood.
Over these things I could not see:
These were the things that bounded me;
And I could touch them with my hand,
Almost, I thought, from where I stand.
And all at once things seemed so small
My breath came short, and scarce at all.
But, sure, the sky is big, I said:
Miles and miles above my head;
So here upon my back I'll lie
And look my fill into the sky.
And so I looked, and, after all,
The sky was not so very tall.
The sky, I said, must somewhere stop,
And—sure enough!—I see the top!
The sky, I thought, is not so grand;
I 'most could touch it with my hand!
And reaching up my hand to try,
I screamed to feel it touch the sky.
I screamed, and—lo!—Infinity
Came down and settled over me;
Forced back my scream into my chest,
Bent back my arm upon my breast,

And, pressing of the Undefined
The definition on my mind,
Held up before my eyes a glass
Through which my shrinking sight did pass
Until it seemed I must behold
Immensity made manifold;
Whispered to me a word whose sound
Deafened the air for worlds around,
And brought unmuffled to my ears
The gossiping of friendly spheres,
The creaking of the tented sky,
The ticking of Eternity.

I saw and heard and knew at last
The How and Why of all things, past,
And present, and forevermore.
The Universe cleft to the core,
Lay open to my probing sense
That, sick'ning, I would fain pluck thence
But could not,—nay! But needs must suck
At the great wound, and could not pluck
My lips away till I had drawn
All venom out.—Ah, fearful pawn!
For my omniscience paid I toll
In infinite remorse of soul.
All sin was of my sinning, all
Atoning mine, and mine the gall
Of all regret. Mine was the weight
Of every brooded wrong, the hate
That stood behind each envious thrust,
Mine every greed, mine every lust.
And all the while for every grief,
Each suffering, I craved relief
With individual desire,—
Craved all in vain! And felt fierce fire
About a thousand people crawl;
Perished with each,—then mourned for all!
A man was starving in Capri;
He moved his eyes and looked at me;
I felt his gaze, I heard his moan,
And knew his hunger as my own.
I saw at sea a great fog bank
Between two ships that struck and sank;
A thousand screams the heavens smote;
And every scream tore through my throat.

No hurt I did not feel, no death
That was not mine; mine each last breath
That, crying, met an answering cry
From the compassion that was I.
All suffering mine, and mine its rod;
Mine, pity like the pity of God.
Ah, awful weight! Infinity
Pressed down upon the finite Me!
My anguished spirit, like a bird,
Beating against my lips I heard;
Yet lay the weight so close about
There was no room for it without.
And so beneath the weight lay I
And suffered death, but could not die.

Long had I lain thus, craving death,
When quietly the earth beneath
Gave way, and inch by inch, so great
At last had grown the crushing weight,
Into the earth I sank till I
Full six feet under ground did lie,
And sank no more,—there is no weight
Can follow here, however great.
From off my breast I felt it roll,
And as it went my tortured soul
Burst forth and fled in such a gust
That all about me swirled the dust.

Deep in the earth I rested now;
Cool is its hand upon the brow
And soft its breast beneath the head
Of one who is so gladly dead.
And all at once, and over all
The pitying rain began to fall:
I lay and heard each pattering hoof
Upon my lowly, thatched roof,
And seemed to love the sound far more
Than ever I had done before.
For rain it hath a friendly sound
To one who's six feet under ground;
And scarce the friendly voice or face:
A grave is such a quiet place.

The rain, I said, is kind to come
And speak to me in my new home.

I would I were alive again
To kiss the fingers of the rain,
To drink into my eyes the shine
Of every slanting silver line,
To catch the freshened, fragrant breeze
From drenched and dripping apple-trees.
For soon the shower will be done,
And then the broad face of the sun
Will laugh above the rain-soaked earth
Until the world with answering mirth
Shakes joyously, and each round drop
Rolls, twinkling, from its grass-blade top.
How can I bear it; buried here,
While overhead the sky grows clear
And blue again after the storm?
O, multi-colored, multiform,
Beloved beauty over me,
That I shall never, never see
Again! Spring-silver, autumn-gold,
That I shall never more behold!
Sleeping your myriad magics through,
Close-sepulchred away from you!
O God, I cried, give me new birth,
And put me back upon the earth!
Upset each cloud's gigantic gourd
And let the heavy rain, down-poured
In one big torrent, set me free,
Washing my grave away from me!

I ceased; and through the breathless hush
That answered me, the far-off rush
Of herald wings came whispering
Like music down the vibrant string
Of my ascending prayer, and—crash!
Before the wild wind's whistling lash
The startled storm-clouds reared on high
And plunged in terror down the sky
And the big rain in one black wave
Fell from the sky and struck my grave.
I know not how such things can be;
I only know there came to me
A fragrance such as never clings
To aught save happy living things;
A sound as of some joyous elf
Singing sweet songs to please himself,

And, through and over everything,
A sense of glad awakening.
The grass, a-tiptoe at my ear,
Whispering to me I could hear;
I felt the rain's cool finger-tips
Brushed tenderly across my lips,
Laid gently on my sealèd sight,
And all at once the heavy night
Fell from my eyes and I could see,—
A drenched and dripping apple-tree,
A last long line of silver rain,
A sky grown clear and blue again.
And as I looked a quickening gust
Of wind blew up to me and thrust
Into my face a miracle
Of orchard-breath, and with the smell,—
I know not how such things can be!—
I breathed my soul back into me.
Ah! Up then from the ground sprang I
And hailed the earth with such a cry
As is not heard save from a man
Who has been dead, and lives again.

About the trees my arms I wound;
Like one gone mad I hugged the ground;
I raised my quivering arms on high;
I laughed and laughed into the sky,
Till at my throat a strangling sob
Caught fiercely, and a great heart-throb
Sent instant tears into my eyes;
Oh God, I cried, no dark disguise
Can e'er hereafter hide from me
Thy radiant identity!
Thou canst not move across the grass
But my quick eyes will see Thee pass,
Nor speak, however silently,
But my hushed voice will answer Thee.
I know the path that tells Thy way
Through the cool eve of every day,
God, I can push the grass apart
And lay my finger on Thy heart!

The world stands out on either side
No wider than the heart is wide;
Above the world is stretched the sky,—

No higher than the soul is high.
The heart can push the sea and land
Farther away on either hand;
The soul can split the sky in two,
And let the face of God shine through.
But East and West will pinch the heart
That can not keep them pushed apart;
And he whose soul is flat—the sky
Will cave in on him by and by.

Bettmann

L'Envoi

RUDYARD KIPLING
(Born December 30, 1865; died January 17, 1936)

When earth's last picture is painted, and the tubes are twisted and
dried,
When the oldest colors have faded, and the youngest critic has died,
We shall rest, and, faith, we shall need it—lie down for an aeon or
two.
Till the Master of All Good Workmen shall set us to work anew!

And those that were good will be happy: they shall sit in a golden
chair;
They shall splash at a ten-league canvas with brushes of comets'
hair;
They shall find real saints to draw from — Magdalene, Peter, and
Paul;
They shall work for an age at a sitting and never be tired at all!

And only the Master shall praise us, and only the Master shall
blame;
And no one shall work for money, and no one shall work for fame;
But each for the joy of the working, and each, in his separate star,
Shall draw the Thing as he sees It for the God of Things as They
Are!

Bettmann

Epilogue to Asolando

ROBERT BROWNING
(Born May 7, 1812; died December 12, 1889)

At the midnight in the silence of the sleep-time,
  When you set your fancies free,
Will they pass to where—by death, fools think, imprisoned—
Low he lies who once so loved you, whom you loved so,
      —Pity me?

Oh to love so, be so loved, yet so mistaken!
  What had I on earth to do
With the slothful, with the mawkish, the unmanly?
Like the aimless, helpless, hopeless, did I drivel
      —Being—who?

One who never turned his back but marched breast forward,
  Never doubted clouds would break,
Never dreamed, though right were worsted, wrong would triumph,
Held we fall to rise, are baffled to fight better,
      Sleep to wake.

No, at noonday in the bustle of man's work-time
  Greet the unseen with a cheer!
Bid him forward, breast and back as either should be,
"Strive and thrive!" cry "Speed,—fight on, fare ever
    There as here!"

By special permission of the Houghton-Mifflin
Co.

In regard to the third stanza of this poem the
Pall Mall Gazette of February 1, 1890, related
this incident: "One evening, just before his
death-illness, the poet was reading this from a
proof to his daughter-in-law and sister. He
said: 'It almost looks like bragging to say this,
and as if I ought to cancel it; but it's the
simple truth; and as it's true, it shall stand.'"

Bettmann

Gettysburg Address

Speech at the Dedication of the National Cemetery at Gettysburg November 19, 1863

ABRAHAM LINCOLN

(Born February 12, 1809; died April 15, 1865)

Fourscore and seven years ago our fathers brought forth upon this continent a new nation, conceived in liberty, and dedicated to the proposition that all men are created equal. Now we are engaged in a great civil war, testing whether that nation, or any nation so conceived and so dedicated, can long endure. We are met on a great battlefield of that war. We have come to dedicate a portion of that field as a final resting-place for those who here gave their lives that that nation might live. It is altogether fitting and proper that we should do this. But in a larger sense we cannot dedicate, we cannot consecrate, we cannot hallow this ground. The brave men, living and dead, who struggled here, have consecrated it far above our poor power to add or detract. The world will little note, nor long remember, what we say here; but it can never forget what they did here. It is for us, the living, rather to be dedicated here to the unfinished work which they who fought here have thus far so nobly advanced. It is rather for us to be here dedicated to the great task remaining before us, that from these honored dead we take increased devotion to that cause for which they gave the last full measure of devotion; that we here highly resolve that these dead shall not have died in vain; that this nation, under God, shall have a new birth of freedom, and that government of the people, by the people, and for the people, shall not perish from the earth.

Executive Mansion
Washington, Nov 21, 1864

To Mrs Bixby, Boston, Mass,

Dear Madam.

I have been shown in the files
of the War Department a statement of the Adjutant
General of Massachusetts that you are the mother of
five sons who have died gloriously on the field of battle
I feel how weak and fruitless must be any word of
mine which should attempt to beguile you from the
grief of a loss so overwhelming But I cannot refrain
from tendering you the consolation that may be found
in the thanks of the republic they died to save I
pray that our Heavenly Father may assuage the anguish
of your bereavement, and leave you only the cherished
memory of the loved and lost, and the solemn pride
that must be yours to have laid so costly a sacrifice
upon the altar of freedom

Yours very sincerely and respectfully
A. Lincoln

On the walls of Brasenose College, Oxford
University, England, this letter of the "rail-
splitter" President hangs as a model of purest
English, rarely, if ever, surpassed.

The Ten Commandments

I

I am the Lord thy God, which have brought thee out of the land of Egypt, out of the house of bondage.

Thou shalt have no other gods before me.

II

Thou shalt not make unto thee any graven image, or any likeness of any thing that is in heaven above, or that is in the earth beneath, or that is in the water under the earth:

Thou shalt not bow down thyself to them, nor serve them: for I the Lord thy God am a jealous God, visiting the iniquity of the fathers upon the children unto the third and fourth generation of them that hate me;

And shewing mercy unto thousands of them that love me, and keep my commandments.

III

Thou shalt not take the name of the lord thy God in vain; for the Lord will not hold him guiltless that taketh his name in vain.

IV

Remember the Sabbath day to keep it holy:

Six days shalt thou labor, and do all thy work:

But the seventh day is the Sabbath of the Lord thy God; in it thou shalt not do any work, thou, nor thy son, nor thy daughter, thy man-servant, nor thy maid-servant, nor thy cattle, nor the stranger that is within thy gates:

For in six days the Lord made heaven and earth, the sea, and all that in them is, and rested the seventh day: wherefore the Lord blessed the Sabbath day, and hallowed it.

V

Honor thy father and thy mother: that thy days may be long upon the land which the Lord thy God giveth thee.

VI

Thou shalt not kill.

VII

Thou shalt not commit adultery.

VIII

Thou shalt not steal.

IX

Thou shalt not bear false witness against thy neighbor.

X

Thou shalt not covet thy neighbor's house, thou shalt not covet thy neighbor's wife, nor his man-servant, nor his maid-servant, nor his ox, nor his ass, nor anything that is thy neighbor's.

Magna Charta

Bettmann

On June 15, 1215, King John met the barons near Runnymeade on the Thames, and granted them the charter which they laid before him.

This charter contains sixty-three articles, some of which were merely temporary; the principles upon which the whole English judicial system is based are these:

"No freeman shall be taken or imprisoned, or disseised*, or outlawed, or banished . . . unless by the lawful judgment of his peers, or by the law of the land."

"We will sell to no man, we will not deny to any man, either justice or right."

Among the most important articles were the two which limited the power of the king in matters of taxation:

"No scutage or aid shall be imposed in our kingdom unless by the general council of our kingdom;"

and

"For the holding of the general council of the kingdom . . . we shall cause to be summoned the archbishops, bishops, abbots, earls, and the greater barons of the realm, singly, by our letters. And furthermore we shall cause to be summoned generally by our sheriffs and bailiffs, all others who hold of us in chief."

*Dispossessed of land.

Bettmann

The War Inevitable, March, 1775

PATRICK HENRY
(Born May 29, 1736; died June 6, 1799)

They tell us, Sir, that we are weak — unable to cope with so formidable an adversary. But when shall we be stronger? Will it be the next week, or the next year? Will it be when we are totally disarmed, and when a British guard shall be stationed in every house? Shall we gather strength by irresolution and inaction? Shall we acquire the means of effectual resistance by lying supinely on our backs, and hugging the delusive phantom of hope, until our enemies shall have bound us hand and foot? Sir, we are not weak, if we make a proper use of those means which the God of nature hath placed in our power.

Three millions of People, armed in the holy cause of liberty, and in such a country as that which we possess, are invincible by any force which our enemy can send against us. Beside, Sir, we shall not fight our battles alone. There is a just God who presides over the destinies of Nations, and who will raise up friends to fight our battles for us. The battle, Sir, is not to the strong alone; it is to the vigilant, the active, the brave. Besides, Sir, we have no election. If we were base enough to desire it, it is now too late to retire from the contest. There is no retreat but in submission and slavery! Our chains are forged! Their clanking may be heard on the plains of Boston! The war is inevitable; and let it come! I repeat, Sir, let it come!

It is in vain, Sir, to extenuate the matter. Gentlemen may cry, Peace, Peace!—but there is no peace. The war is actually begun! The next gale that sweeps from the North will bring to our ears the clash of resounding arms! Our brethren are already in the field! Why stand we here idle? What is it that Gentlemen wish? What would they have? Is life so dear, or peace so sweet, as to be purchased at the price of chains and slavery? Forbid it, Almighty God! I know not what course others may take; but as for me, give me liberty or give me death!

The Declaration of Independence
In Congress, July 4th, 1776

The Unanimous Declaration of the
Thirteen United States of America

When, in the course of human events, it becomes necessary for one people to dissolve the political bands which have connected them with another, and to assume, among the powers of the earth, the separate and equal station to which the laws of nature and of nature's God entitle them, a decent respect to the opinions of mankind requires that they should declare the causes which impel them to the separation.

We hold these truths to be self-evident: that all men are created equal; that they are endowed by their Creator with certain inalienable rights; that among these are life, liberty, and the pursuit of happiness. That to secure these rights, governments are instituted among men, deriving their just powers from the consent of the governed; that whenever any form of government becomes destructive of these ends it is the right of the people to alter or to abolish it, and to institute a new government, laying its foundation on such principles, and organizing its powers in such form, as to them shall seem most likely to effect their safety and happiness. Prudence, indeed, will dictate, that governments long established should not be changed for light and transient causes; and accordingly all experience hath shown, that mankind are more disposed to suffer, while evils are sufferable, than to right themselves by abolishing the forms to which they are accustomed. But when a long train of abuses and usurpations, pursuing invariably the same object, evinces a design to reduce them under absolute despotism, it is their right, it is their duty, to throw off such government, and to provide new guards for their future security. Such has been the patient sufferance of these colonies; and such is now the necessity which constrains them to alter their former system of government. The history of the present king of Great Britain is a history of repeated injuries and usurpations, all having in direct object the establishment of an absolute tyranny over these states. To prove this, let facts be submitted to a candid world.

He has refused his assent to laws the most wholesome and necessary for the public good.

He has forbidden his governors to pass laws of immediate and pressing importance, unless suspended in their operation till his assent should be obtained; and when so suspended, he has utterly neglected to attend to them.

He has refused to pass other laws for the accommodation of large districts of people, unless those people would relinquish the right of representation in the legislature—a right inestimable to them, and formidable to tyrants only.

He has called together legislative bodies at places unusual, uncomfortable, and distant from the depository of their public records, for the sole purpose of fatiguing them into compliance with his measures.

He has dissolved representative houses repeatedly, for opposing, with manly firmness, his invasions on the rights of the people.

He has refused, for a long time after such dissolutions, to cause others to be elected; whereby the legislative powers, incapable of annihilation, have returned to the people at large, for their exercise, the state remaining in the meantime exposed to all the dangers of invasion from without, and convulsions within.

He has endeavored to prevent the population of these states; for that purpose obstructing the laws for naturalization of foreigners; refusing to pass others to encourage their migration hither, and raising the conditions of new appropriations of lands.

He has obstructed the administration of justice, by refusing his assent to laws for establishing judiciary powers.

He has made judges dependent on his will alone, for the tenure of their offices, and the amount and payment of their salaries.

He has erected a multitude of new offices, and sent hither swarms of officers, to harass our people, and eat out their substance.

He has kept among us, in times of peace, standing armies, without the consent of our legislature.

He has affected to render the military independent of, and superior to, the civil power.

He has combined with others to subject us to a jurisdiction foreign to our constitution, and unacknowledged by our laws; giving his assent to their acts of pretended legislation:

For quartering large bodies of armed troops among us:

For protecting them, by a mock trial, from punishment for any murders which they should commit on the inhabitants of these states:

For cutting off our trade with all parts of the world:

For imposing taxes on us without our consent:

For depriving us, in many cases, of the benefits of trial by jury:

For transporting us beyond seas to be tried for pretended offences:

For abolishing the free system of English laws in a neighboring province, establishing therein an arbitrary government, and enlarging its boundaries, so as to render it at once an example and fit instrument for introducing the same absolute rule into these colonies:

For taking away our charters, abolishing our most valuable laws, and altering, fundamentally, the forms of our governments:

For suspending our own legislatures, and declaring themselves invested with power to legislate for us in all cases whatsoever.

He has abdicated government here, by declaring us out of his protection and waging war against us.

He has plundered our seas, ravaged our coasts, burnt our towns and destroyed the lives of our people.

He is at this time transporting large armies of foreign mercenaries to complete the works of death, desolation, and tyranny, already begun with circumstances of cruelty and perfidy scarcely paralleled in the most barbarous ages, and totally unworthy the head of a civilized nation.

He has constrained our fellow-citizens, taken captive on the high seas, to bear arms against their country, to become the executioners of their friends and brethren, or to fall themselves by their hands.

He has excited domestic insurrections among us, and has endeavored to bring on the inhabitants of our frontiers the merciless Indian savages, whose known rule of warfare is an undistinguished destruction of all ages, sexes, and conditions.

In every stage of these oppressions we have petitioned for redress in the most humble terms; our repeated petitions have been answered only by repeated injury. A prince whose character is thus marked by every act which may define a tyrant is unfit to be the ruler of a free people.

Nor have we been wanting in attentions to our British brethren. We have warned them, from time to time, of attempts by their legislature to extend an unwarrantable jurisdiction over us. We have reminded them of the circumstances of our emigration and settlement here. We have appealed to their native justice and magnanimity, and we have conjured them by the ties of our common kindred to disavow these usurpations, which would inevitably interrupt our connections and correspondence. They, too, have been deaf to the voice of justice and consanguinity. We must, therefore, acquiesce in the necessity which denounces our separation, and hold them, as we hold the rest of mankind, enemies in war, in peace friends.

We, therefore, the representatives of the United States of America, in General Congress assembled, appealing to the Supreme Judge of the world for the rectitude of our intentions, do, in the name and by the authority of the good people of these colonies, solemnly publish and declare that these United Colonies are, and of right ought to be, free and independent States; that they are absolved from all allegiance to the British crown, and that all political connection between them and the State of Great Britain is, and ought to be, totally dissolved; and that, as free and independent States, they have full power to levy war, conclude peace, contract alliances, establish commerce, and to do all other acts and things which independent States may of right do. And for the support of this declaration, with a firm reliance on the protection of Divine Providence, we mutually pledge to each other our lives, our fortunes, and our sacred honor.

Signed by order and in behalf of the Congress.

JOHN HANCOCK, President.

Attested, CHARLES THOMPSON, Secretary.

NEW HAMPSHIRE.
Josiah Bartlett,
William Whipple,
Matthew Thornton.

RHODE ISLAND.
Stephen Hopkins,
William Ellery.

NEW YORK.
William Floyd,
Phillip Livingston,
Francis Lewis,
Lewis Morris.

MASSACHUSETTS BAY.
Samuel Adams,
John Adams,
Robert Treat Paine,
Elbridge Gerry.

CONNECTICUT.
Roger Sherman,
Samuel Huntington,
William Williams,
Oliver Wolcott.

NEW JERSEY.
Richard Stockton,
John Witherspoon,
Francis Hopkinson,
John Hart,
Abraham Clark.

PENNSYLVANIA.
Robert Morris,
Benjamin Rush,
Benjamin Franklin,
John Morton,
George Clymer,

James Smith,
George Taylor,
James Wilson,
George Ross.

VIRGINIA.
George Wythe,
Richard Henry Lee,
Thomas Jefferson,
Benjamin Harrison,
Thomas Nelson, Jr.,
Francis Lightfoot Lee,
Carter Braxton.

SOUTH CAROLINA.
Edward Rutledge,
Thomas Heyward, Jr.,
Thomas Lynch, Jr.,
Arthur Middleton.

DELAWARE.
Caesar Rodney,
George Read,
Thomas M'kean.

MARYLAND
Samuel Chase,
William Paca,
Thomas Stone,
Charles Carroll of Carrollton.

NORTH CAROLINA.
William Hooper,
Joseph Hewes,
John Penn.

GEORGIA.
Button Gwinnett,
Lyman Hall,
George Walton.

Index

PROSE

Index of Authors